Come Home at Once

GUY ATKINS

www.transworldbooks.co.uk

Come Home at Once

GUY ATKINS

www.transworldbooks.co.uk

Come Home at Once

GUY ATKINS

BANTAM PRESS

LONDON · TORONTO · SYDNEY · AUCKLAND · JOHANNESBURG

TRANSWORLD PUBLISHERS
61–63 Uxbridge Road, London W5 5SA
A Random House Group Company
www.transworldbooks.co.uk

First published in Great Britain in 2014 by Bantam Press
an imprint of Transworld Publishers

A CIP catalogue record for this book
is available from the British Library.

ISBN 9780593074145

Addresses for Random House Group Ltd companies outside the UK
can be found at: www.randomhouse.co.uk
The Random House Group Ltd Reg. No. 954009

Typeset in Minion

Printed and bound in China

2 4 6 8 10 9 7 5 3 1

In memory of
Margaret Atkins

Introduction

Villiers Street runs out of the back of Embankment Tube station in London, away from the Thames and up to Charing Cross railway station. Lined with cafés, pubs and making-working-life-easy shops, it serves as a base for the city's largest accountancy firm and is part of the route for tourists making their way from the South Bank to the West End. During the week, a gym, a shoe repair shop and a newsagent are on hand to maintain the pace of the office worker's day. Coffee is also in good supply: Starbucks alone has two branches on the street. At the weekend, while there are fewer suits and laptops, the area is no less busy. Shoppers, sightseers and people off to the theatre hurry up and down the street.

On Saturdays, and only on Saturdays, by the Starbucks nearest the river, a fire escape is propped open with a blue sandwich board. Passing the board marked 'Charing X Collectors Fair', the hustle of Villiers Street fades away. A corridor leads you to a flight of concrete steps, which in turn takes you down to a car park beneath street level. Here, under bare fluorescent strips, are typically twenty or thirty market stalls of carefully ordered ephemera: stamps, cigarette cards and vintage football programmes are laid out on wooden trestle tables and traded. On arriving, I make my way straight to the back, to the postcard dealers.

For the next couple of hours I will trawl through each dealer's stock, hoping to locate items to add to my collection of Edwardian postcard messages. Over the past ten years, I've become hooked on collecting messages from the decade or so before the First World War, from what was the postcard's 'Golden Age'. On the pages that follow are the most intriguing and beautiful cards I've managed to find.

It was the message on the card from which this book takes its title that got me started. I found it while flicking through a tray of old cards in a bric-à-brac shop in the Lake District. On the front is a picture of 'The Cross' in the market town of Rothbury, in Northumberland. Empty of people and tinted with dreary pastel shades, the image could only appeal to someone who already knows the town.

Yet on the back is a message that turns the card into a wholly compelling object. Sent to a Miss Emerson on 21 December 1904, care of Mr Bollam, it reads:

> 'Come home at once, all is forgiven. We have not had any news from father. There is heaps of m---y waiting for you to spend. Surely after that you could not stay away.'

Come home at once. Ten years on, I can still remember the rush of holding the card for the first time, and how I struggled to process all the questions that came to mind. What had Miss Emerson done that needed forgiving? Did she go home after receiving the postcard? Did the card even reach her? Who sent it? Why had the sender written a postcard and not a letter? And how, a century later, had the card ended up on sale in the Lake District for 50p?

Over the years, I've dreamt up many versions of the card's provenance, though none has really stuck: attempts at a definitive account have been thwarted by the absence of Miss Emerson and Mr Bollam from census records; and whenever I show the card to friends, they invariably see alternative possibilities, possibilities that unsettle my latest theory. Yet rather than this being a problem, I have come to realize that it is because of its unanswered questions that the card is so special – it defiantly resists, in the words of Walter Benjamin, 'being shot through with explanation.'[i]

At the same time as recognizing the impossibility of getting close to the dialogue of which the card was a part, I have found myself drawn into finding out more about the history of postcards, about some of the card's context: why Edwardian postcards seem so different from cards from other periods, why at markets they represent the majority of those on offer.

The biggest surprise was discovering the effectiveness of the Post Office in the Edwardian era. Today, sending a postcard is a signal of not caring about the timeliness of a message. Then, speed was part of a postcard's essence. Incredibly, there were up to six deliveries a day in British towns and cities – twelve in the centre of London – making it possible to send a postcard or letter in the morning and to receive a reply later the same day. Consequently, with the telephone not yet widely available, the postcard was used for much more than wish-you-were-here greetings. As you will see from the cards in this book, despite their open form, postcards carried messages on every aspect of life: urgent requests for help, declarations of love, impish one-liners about well-known actors, even news of dying relatives. In short, the Edwardian postcard was the text or tweet of its day.

And sending a card was cheap, which made postcards accessible to all but the very poor. The cost of postage was half that of a letter, and efficient printing meant that postcards were produced cheaply enough for people to experiment with them, combining words with images like never before. In an obvious parallel to how people play with the limits of today's social media, senders enjoyed testing the form of the postcard. It was common practice to employ codes, to write backwards or in shorthand, or to use the angle of a card's stamp to show affection towards the recipient (see page 220 for more on 'The Language of Stamps'). The more affluent even sent cards made from personal photographs. Such play was especially evident at the beginning of the Edwardian era, when the postcard's form was still so novel: only in 1894 had the Post Office permitted people to send picture postcards at the halfpenny rate, and only from 1902 were cards published with space for both the address and the message on the back – previously one side was reserved entirely for the address. Given rising levels of literacy and the informality encouraged by postcards, it has been argued that the 'Golden Age' of postcards helped democratize writing in Britain.[ii] What is certain is the postcard's popularity: by the start of the First World War the Post Office was delivering nearly a billion cards a year.

This all means that a market like Charing Cross represents a kind of archive of everyday life at the beginning of the twentieth century. Although eventually the car park's poor lighting will induce a headache of sorts, time spent there leafing through boxes of postcards, deciphering ink and pencil scrawls, is invariably both moving and humbling. Sometimes I'm overwhelmed simply by how the cards offer material connections to so many forgotten conversations, other times by how they evidence the enormous inequality in people's circumstances. And after the market, whenever I pick up one of the albums in which I store my collection, the cards inevitably prompt further reflection – not least, why some messages touch me more than others. In his 1909 city guide, *Adventures in London*, writer James Douglas described postcards as 'a candid revelation of our pursuits and pastimes, our customs and costumes, our morals and manners'. He predicted how people 'will fasten upon the Picture Postcard as the best guide to the spirit of the Edwardian Era … they will reconstruct our age from the strange hieroglyphs and pictures that time has spared.' [iii] What he did not foresee, however, was how these short, informal, open messages would seem so oddly of our own time, too.

---

[i] Walter Benjamin, 'The Storyteller' in *Illuminations*, ed. Hannah Arendt (London: Pimlico, 1999), 89

[ii] Julia Gillen and Nigel Hall, 'Edwardian Postcards: Illuminating Ordinary Writing' in *The Anthropology of Writing*, ed. David Barton and Uta Papen (London: Continuum, 2010), 169

[iii] James Douglas, *Adventures in London* (London: Cassell and Company, 1909), 377

The Cross, Front Street, Rothbury.

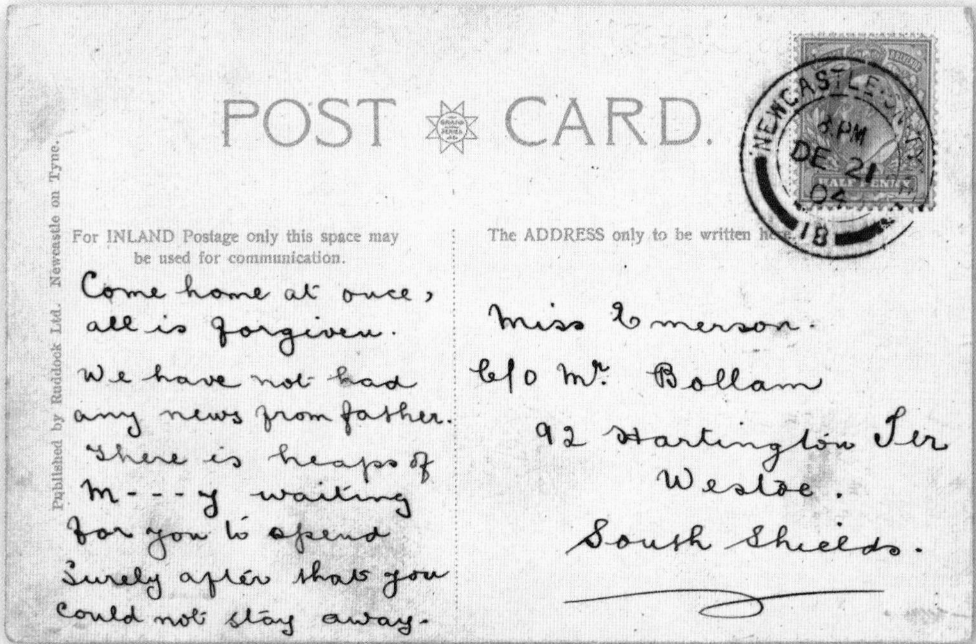

POST CARD.

Published by Ruddock Ltd. Newcastle on Tyne.

NEWCASTLE-ON-TY
3 PM
DE 21
04
18

For INLAND Postage only this space may be used for communication.

Come home at once,
all is forgiven.
We have not had
any news from father.
There is heaps of
M---y waiting
for you to spend
Surely after that you
could not stay away.

The ADDRESS only to be written here.

Miss Emerson.
C/o Mr. Bollam
92 Hartington Ter
Westoe.
South Shields.

22686 Tunbridge Wells. The Common.

POST CARD
THIS SPACE AS WELL AS THE BACK MAY NOW BE USED FOR COMMUNICATION.
INLAND POSTAGE ONLY
THE ADDRESS ONLY TO BE WRITTEN HERE
NO 17
05
DO YOU KNOW.
WHAT.HAPPE
NED.NINETE
EN. YEARS.
AGO. DEAR
MR. C. G. BLUNDELL
CLIFFORDS. STORES
KNOCKHOLT
KENT

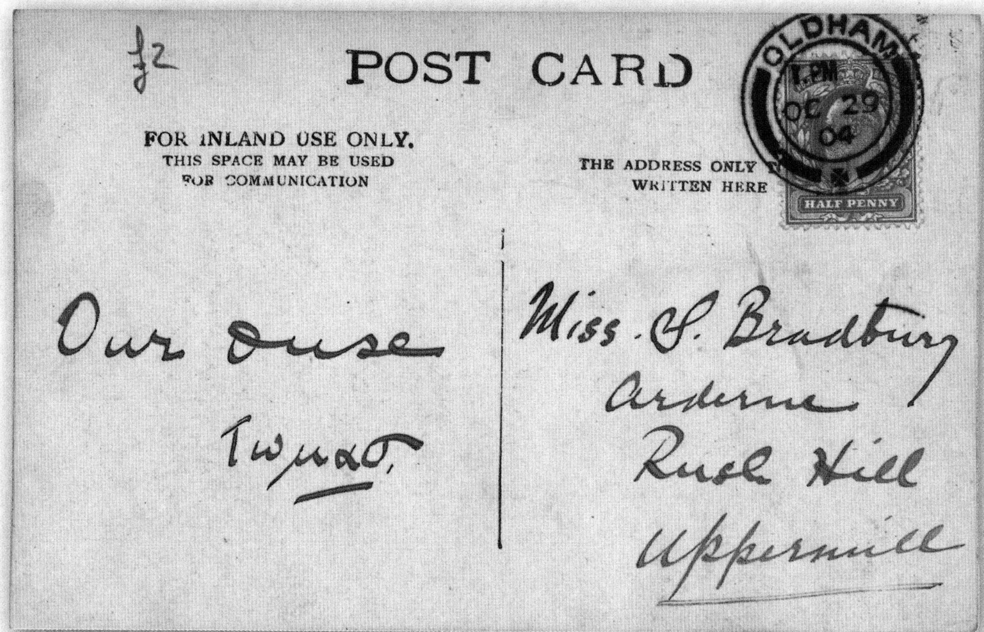

f2

POST CARD

OLDHAM
1 PM
OC 29
04

HALF PENNY

FOR INLAND USE ONLY.
THIS SPACE MAY BE USED
FOR COMMUNICATION

THE ADDRESS ONLY TO BE
WRITTEN HERE

Our ouse

Twyno.

Miss S. Bradbury
Ardenne
Rush Hill
Uppermill

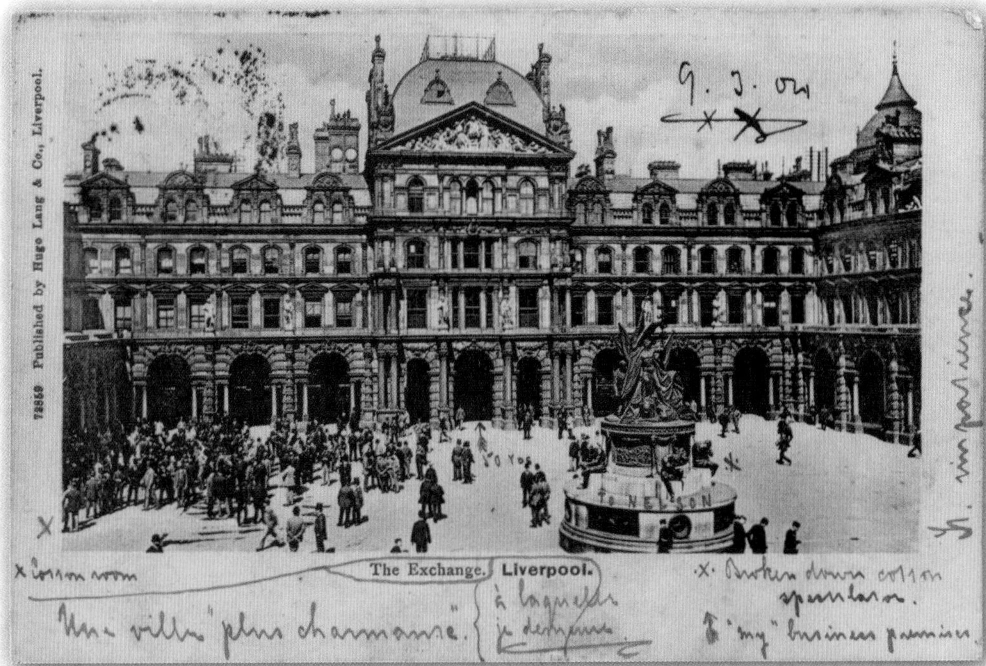
72859 Published by Hugo Lang & Co., Liverpool.
The Exchange. Liverpool.
TO NELSON
9. I. 04
x Cotton room
Une ville "plus charmante."
à laquelle je demeure
·x· Broken down cotton speculators.
"my" business premises

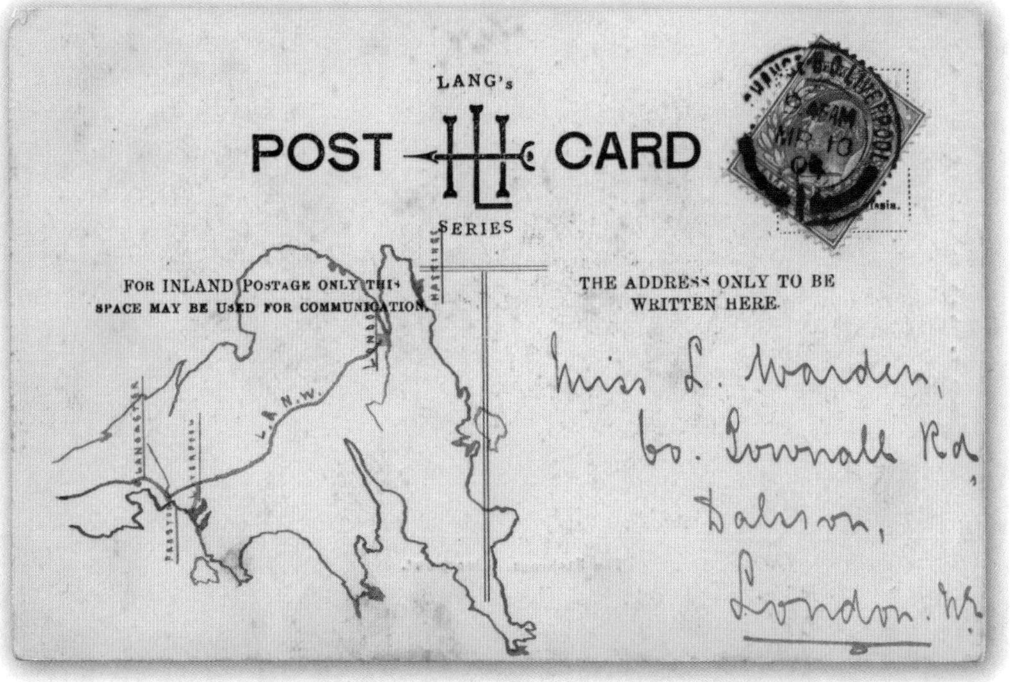
LANG's
POST CARD
SERIES
FOR INLAND POSTAGE ONLY THIS SPACE MAY BE USED FOR COMMUNICATION.
THE ADDRESS ONLY TO BE WRITTEN HERE.
L. & N. W.
Miss L. Warden,
60. Pownall Rd,
Dalston,
London. N.

KENNINGTON, S.O.
10.45PM
JA 17
11
"One of the Workers"
W.E.P.
1911

POST CARD
TO BE USED FOR WRITTEN OR PRINTED MATTER.
ONLY THE ADDRESS TO BE WRITTEN HERE.
KENNINGTON, S.O.S.E.
10.45PM
JA 17
11
5
Miss E. Johnson
129 Kennington Pk Rd
Kennington
S.E.

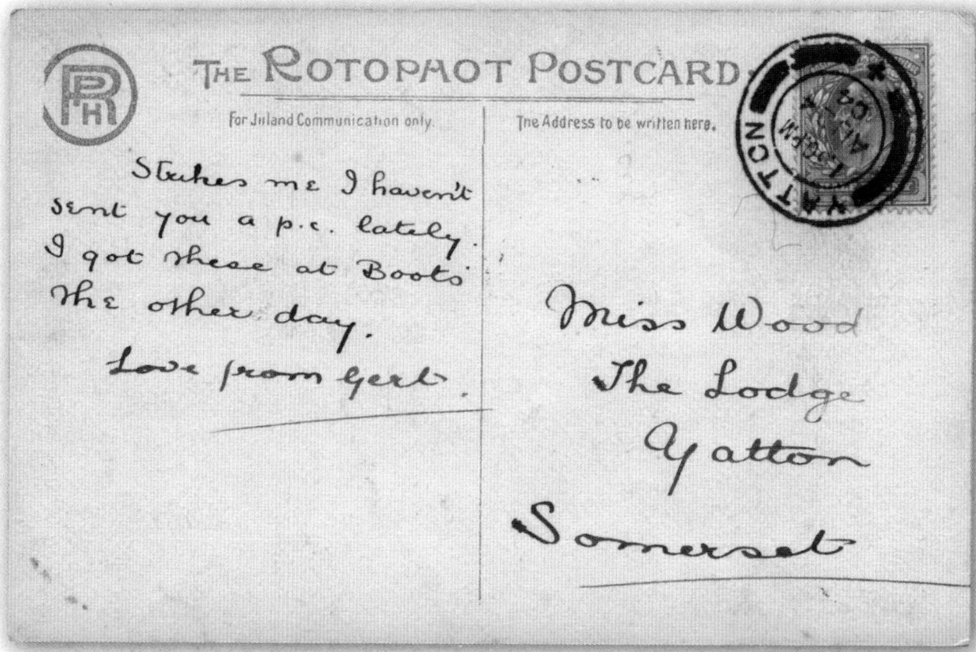
THE ROTOPHOT POSTCARD
For Inland Communication only.
The Address to be written here.
YATTON
Strikes me I haven't sent you a p.c. lately. I got these at Boots' the other day.
Love from Gert.
Miss Wood
The Lodge
Yatton
Somerset

WALTHAM ABBEY.

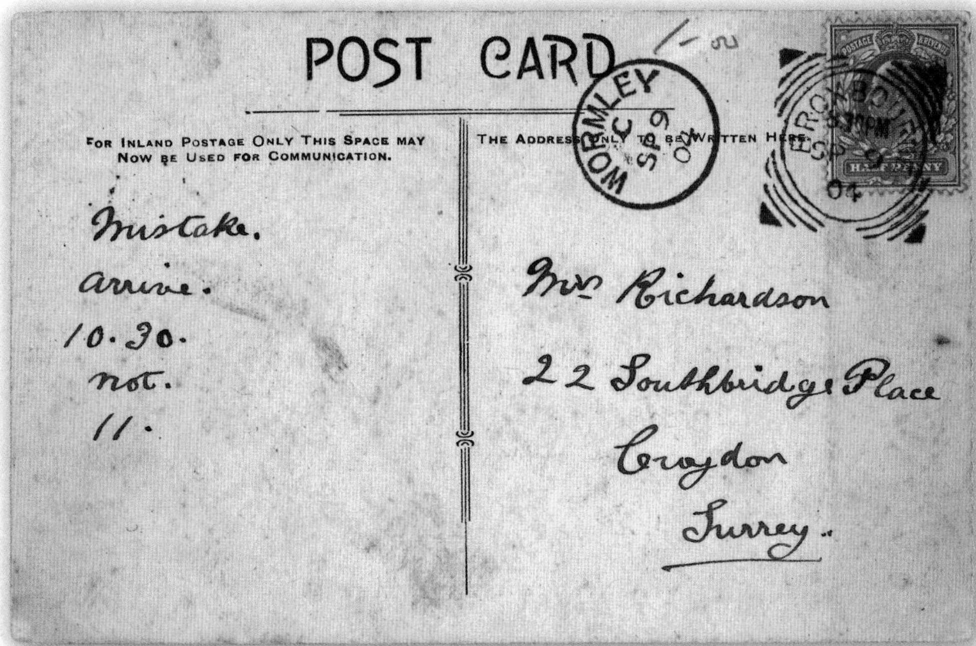
POST CARD
For Inland Postage Only This Space May Now be Used for Communication.
The Address Only to be Written Here.
WORMLEY C SP 9 04
BROXBOURNE 8.30 PM SP 9 04
POSTAGE REVENUE HALF PENNY
Mistake.
arrive.
10.30.
not.
11.
Mrs Richardson
22 Southbridge Place
Croydon
Surrey.

The Central Arch and Meat Market

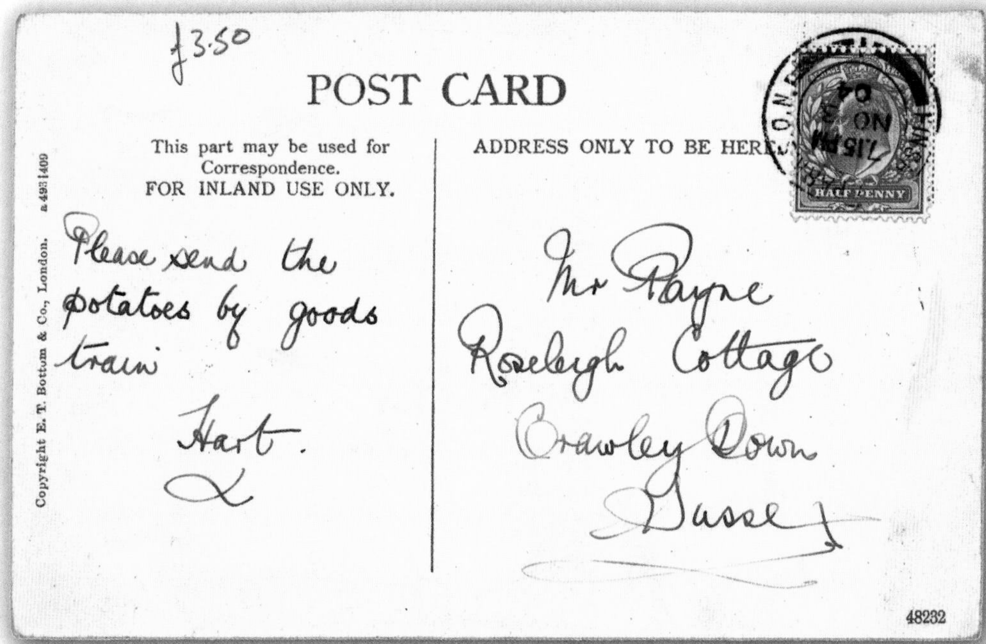

£3.50

POST CARD

This part may be used for
Correspondence.
FOR INLAND USE ONLY.

ADDRESS ONLY TO BE HERE

HALF PENNY

Copyright E. T. Bottom & Co., London. a 493|409

Please send the
potatoes by goods
train

Hart.

Mr Payne
Roseleigh Cottage
Crawley Down
Sussex

48232

GIANTS CAUSEWAY, LADIES WISHING ROCK
Copyright. F. F. & Co.

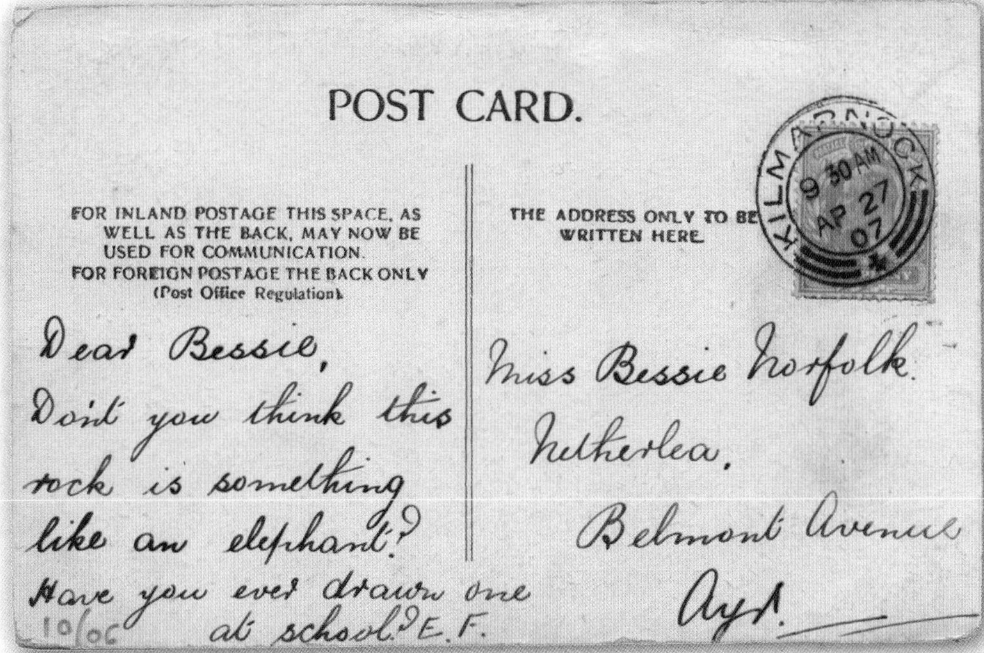

POST CARD.

FOR INLAND POSTAGE THIS SPACE, AS WELL AS THE BACK, MAY NOW BE USED FOR COMMUNICATION.
FOR FOREIGN POSTAGE THE BACK ONLY
(Post Office Regulation).

THE ADDRESS ONLY TO BE WRITTEN HERE.

KILMARNOCK
9 30 AM
AP 27
07

Dear Bessie,
Don't you think this
rock is something
like an elephant?
Have you ever drawn one
10/06 at school? E.F.

Miss Bessie Norfolk.
Netherlea.
Belmont Avenue
Ayr.

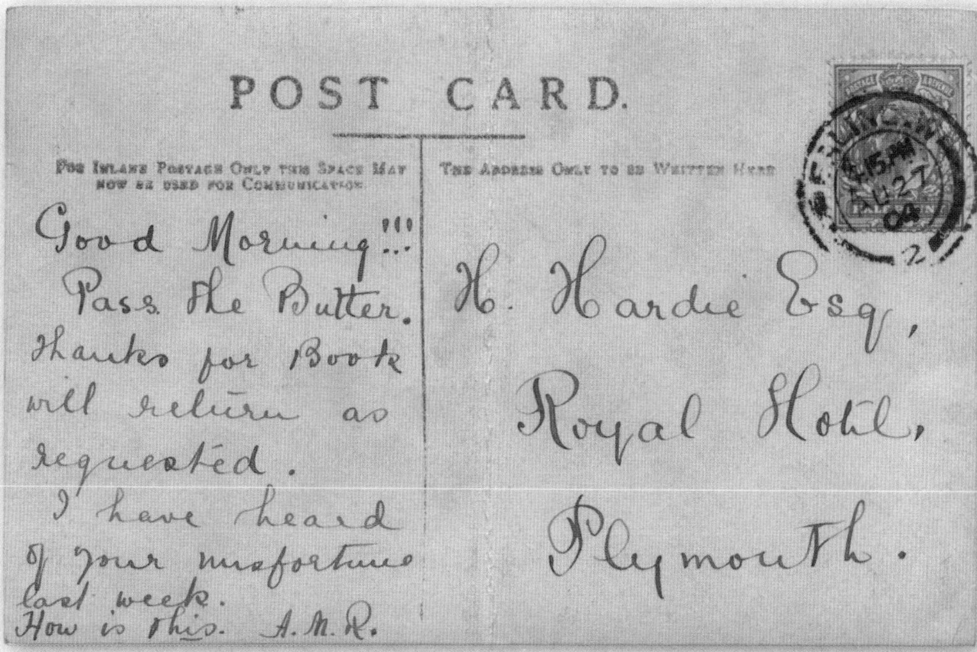

POST CARD.

FOR INLAND POSTAGE ONLY THIS SPACE MAY NOW BE USED FOR COMMUNICATION

Good Morning!!!
Pass the Butter.
Thanks for Book
will return as
requested.
I have heard
of your misfortune
last week.
How is this. A.M.R.

THE ADDRESS ONLY TO BE WRITTEN HERE

H. Hardie Esq,
Royal Hotel,
Plymouth.

St. Michaels and All Angels, Stoke Newington Common.
C. J. & A. Algar, 180 Stoke Newington Road, N.

£8-50

POST CARD

FOR INLAND POSTAGE ONLY THIS SPACE MAY BE USED FOR COMMUNICATION

THE ADDRESS ONLY TO BE WRITTEN HERE

JUL 24 30 AM 05

POSTAGE REVENUE HALF PENNY

Printed in Saxony

Dear Evie

Will you be at Dalston this evening at 6.20 as I want to see you very specially

Yours ever

Edie.

Miss E. A. Ridewood.

24 Bayston Rd.

Stokenewington.

N.

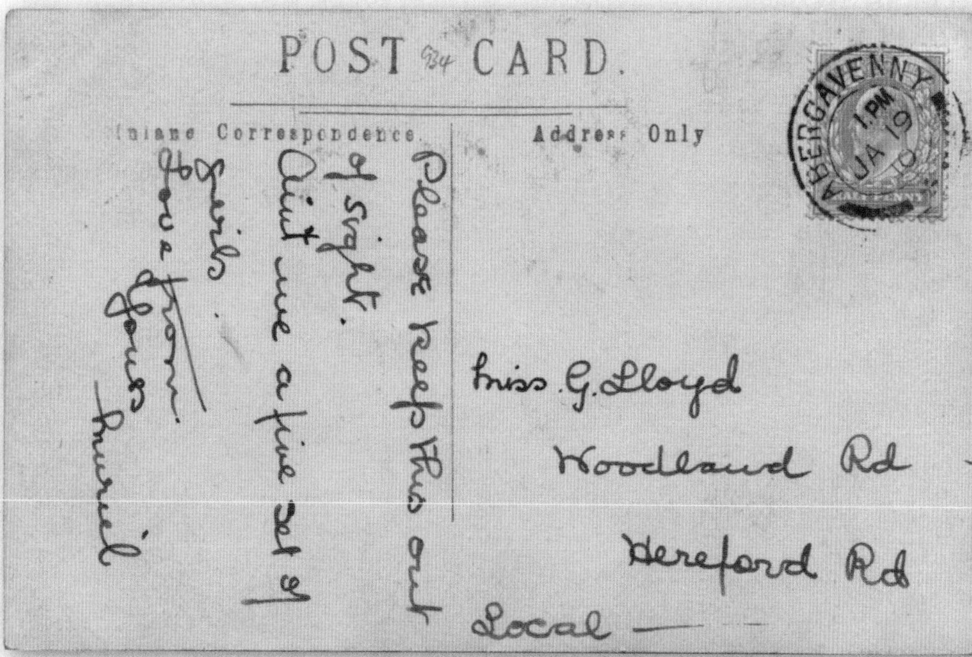
POST CARD.

Inland Correspondence. | Address Only

Please keep this out
of sight.
Ain't we a fine set of
girls.
From
Your
Muriel

ABERGAVENNY 1 PM JA 19 10

Miss G. Lloyd
Woodland Rd
Hereford Rd
Local

Looe Harbour.

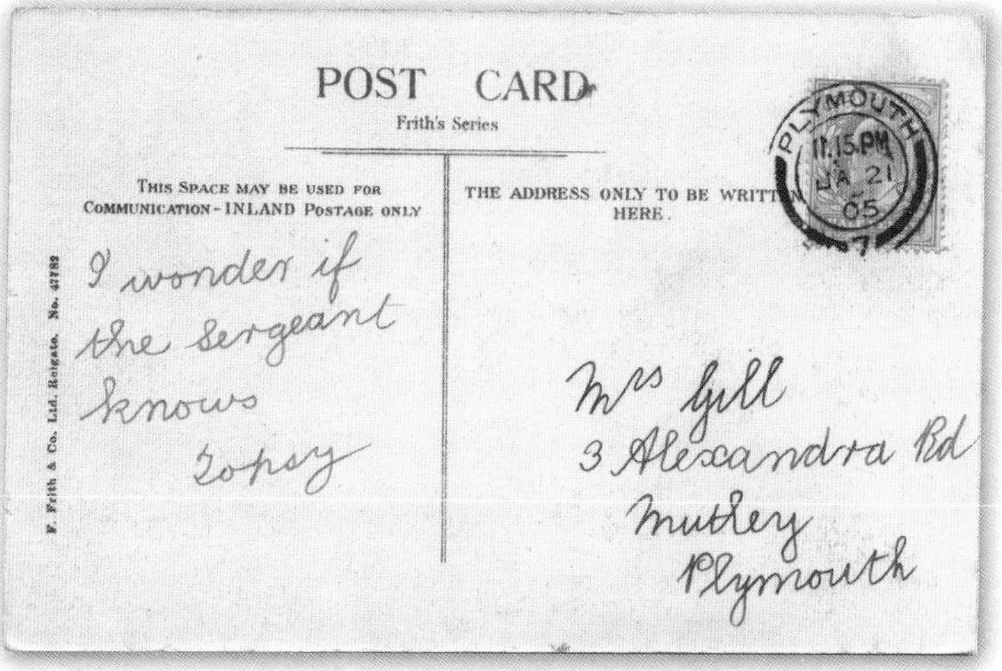
POST CARD
Frith's Series
THIS SPACE MAY BE USED FOR COMMUNICATION - INLAND POSTAGE ONLY
THE ADDRESS ONLY TO BE WRITTEN HERE.
PLYMOUTH
11.15 PM
JA 21
05
7
F. Frith & Co. Ltd. Reigate. No. 47782
I wonder if the Sergeant knows
Topsy
Mrs Gill
3 Alexandra Rd
Mutley
Plymouth

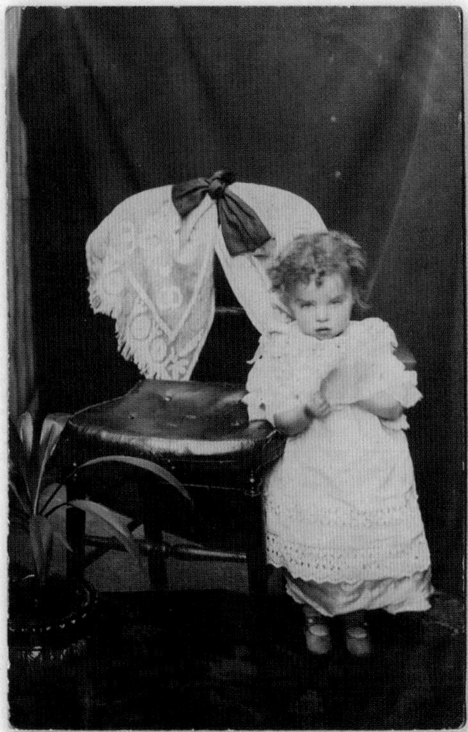

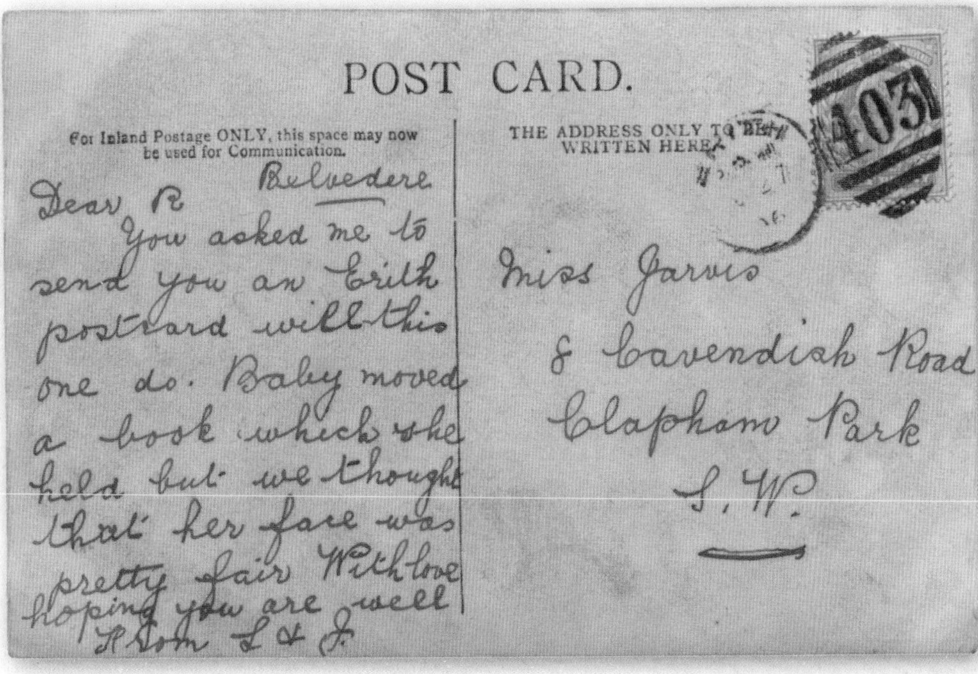

POST CARD.

For Inland Postage ONLY, this space may now be used for Communication.

Belvedere

Dear R

You asked me to send you an Erith postcard will this one do. Baby moved a book which she held but we thought that her face was pretty fair With love hoping you are well

From L & J.

THE ADDRESS ONLY TO BE WRITTEN HERE.

403

Miss Jarvis

8 Cavendish Road

Clapham Park

S.W.

WIMBLEDON BROADWAY.

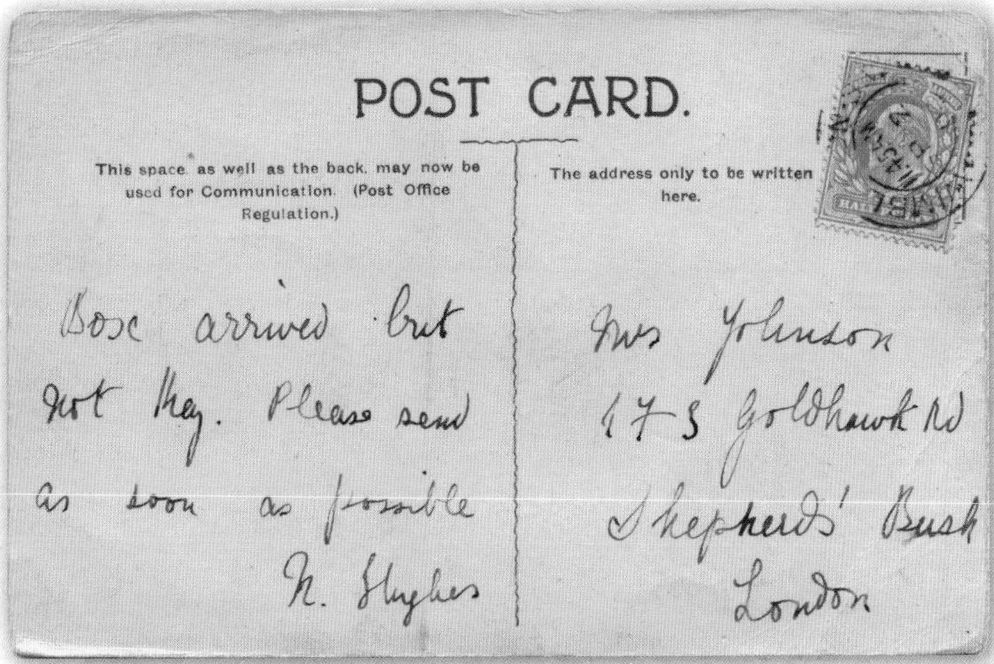
POST CARD.

This space as well as the back, may now be used for Communication. (Post Office Regulation.)

The address only to be written here.

Box arrived but not Key. Please send as soon as possible

N. Hughes

Mrs Johnson
175 Goldhawk Rd
Shepherds' Bush
London

Regent-Street
LONDON.

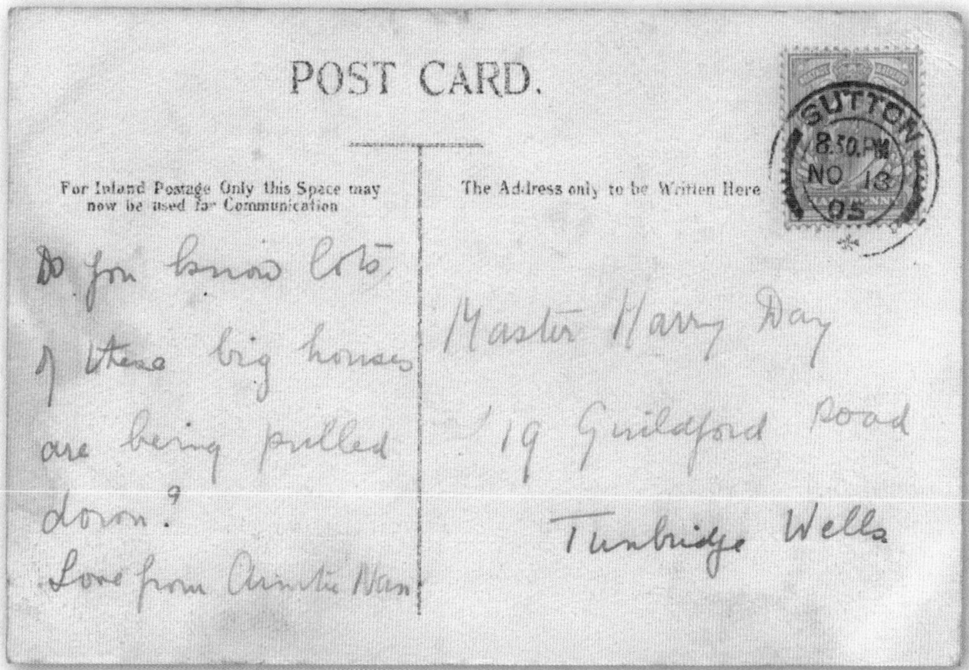

POST CARD.

SUTTON
8.30 PM
NO 13
05

For Inland Postage Only this Space may now be used for Communication

Do you know lots
of these big houses
are being pulled
down?
Love from Auntie Nan

The Address only to be Written Here

Master Harry Day
19 Guildford Road
Tunbridge Wells

THE FIRE AT GADDESDEN PLACE, FEB. 1ST 1905.
DOWNER. COPYRIGHT.

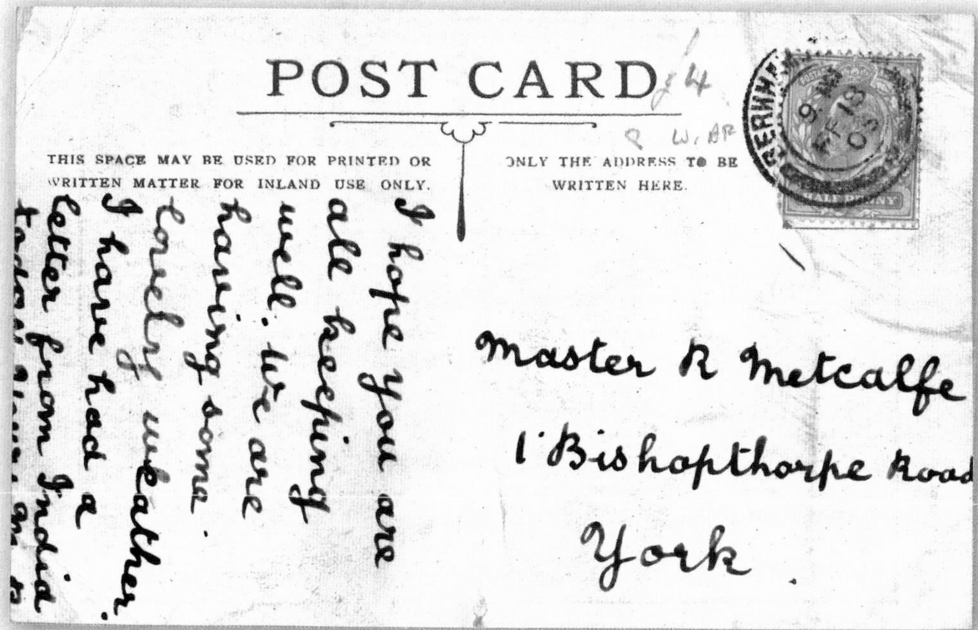
POST CARD
THIS SPACE MAY BE USED FOR PRINTED OR WRITTEN MATTER FOR INLAND USE ONLY.
ONLY THE ADDRESS TO BE WRITTEN HERE.
I hope you are all keeping well. We are having some lovely weather. I have had a letter from India
Master R Metcalfe
1 Bishopthorpe Road
York

THE RUINS OF GADDESDEN PLACE AFTER THE FATAL FIRE OF FEB. 1ST 1905.
DOWNER, PHOTO.

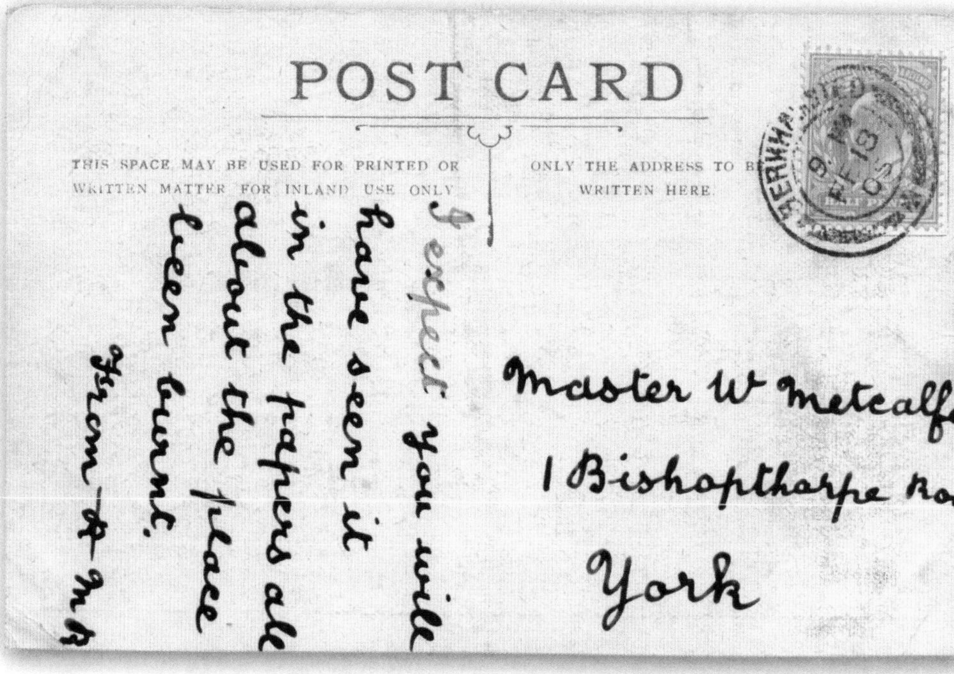
POST CARD
THIS SPACE MAY BE USED FOR PRINTED OR WRITTEN MATTER FOR INLAND USE ONLY
ONLY THE ADDRESS TO BE WRITTEN HERE.
I expect you will
have seen it
in the papers all
about the place
been burnt.
From A M
Master W Metcalfe
1 Bishopthorpe Ro
York

13901.
Old Priory Church, Brecon.

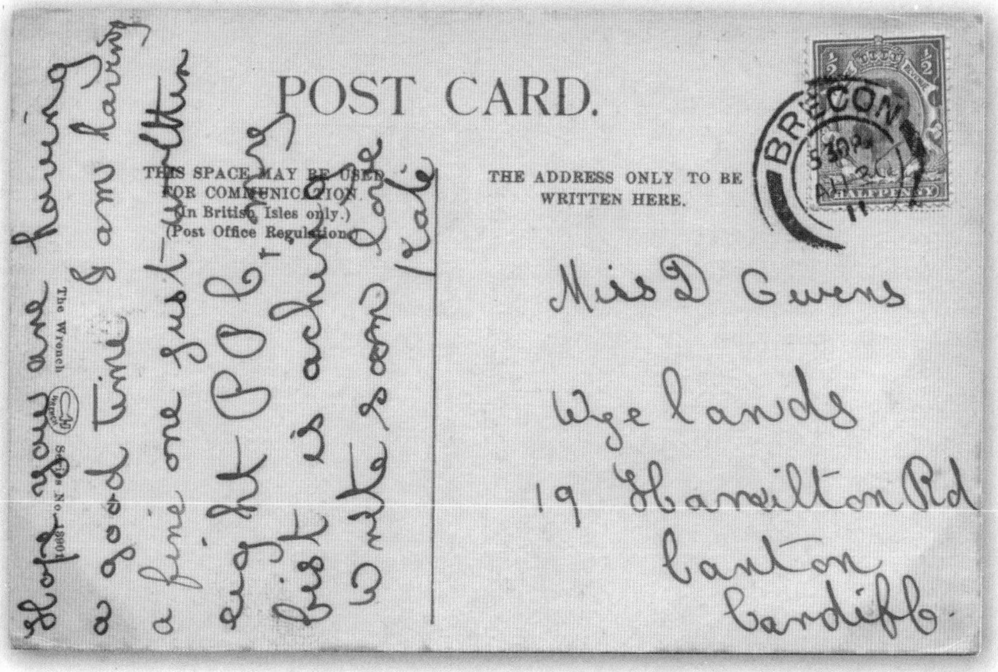
POST CARD.
THIS SPACE MAY BE USED FOR COMMUNICATION. (In British Isles only.) (Post Office Regulations)
THE ADDRESS ONLY TO BE WRITTEN HERE.
BRECON
The Wrench
Hope you are having a good time
Wyelands
19 Hamilton Rd
Canton
Cardiff.

Loving Greetings
The Gentle Art of Boating.

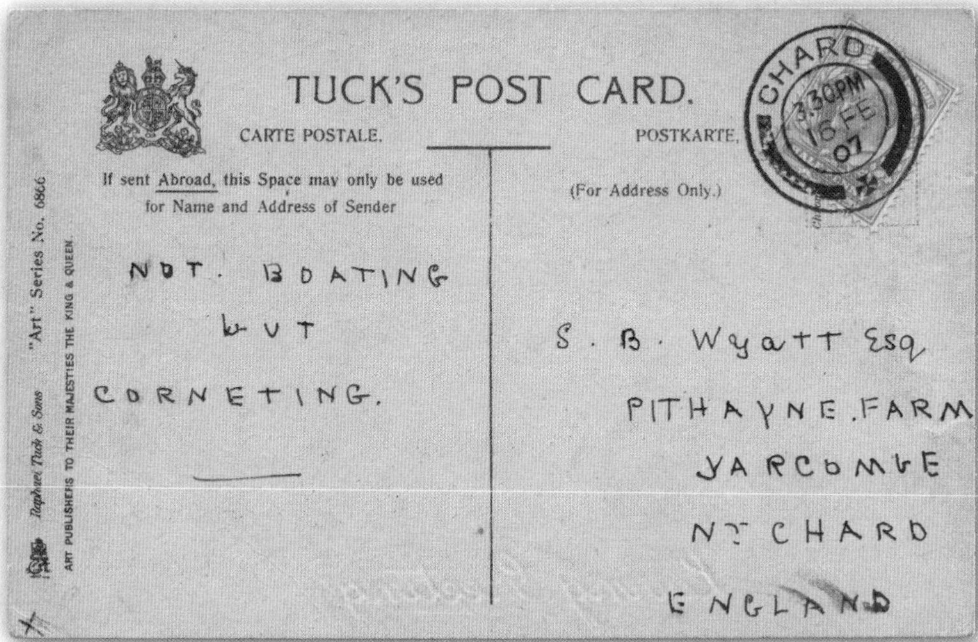
TUCK'S POST CARD.
CARTE POSTALE.
POSTKARTE,
If sent Abroad, this Space may only be used
for Name and Address of Sender
(For Address Only.)
CHARD
3.30PM
16 FE
07
NOT. BOATING
BUT
CORNETING.
S. B. Wyatt Esq
PITHAYNE.FARM
YARCOMBE
NR CHARD
ENGLAND
Raphael Tuck & Sons "Art" Series No. 6866
ART PUBLISHERS TO THEIR MAJESTIES THE KING & QUEEN.

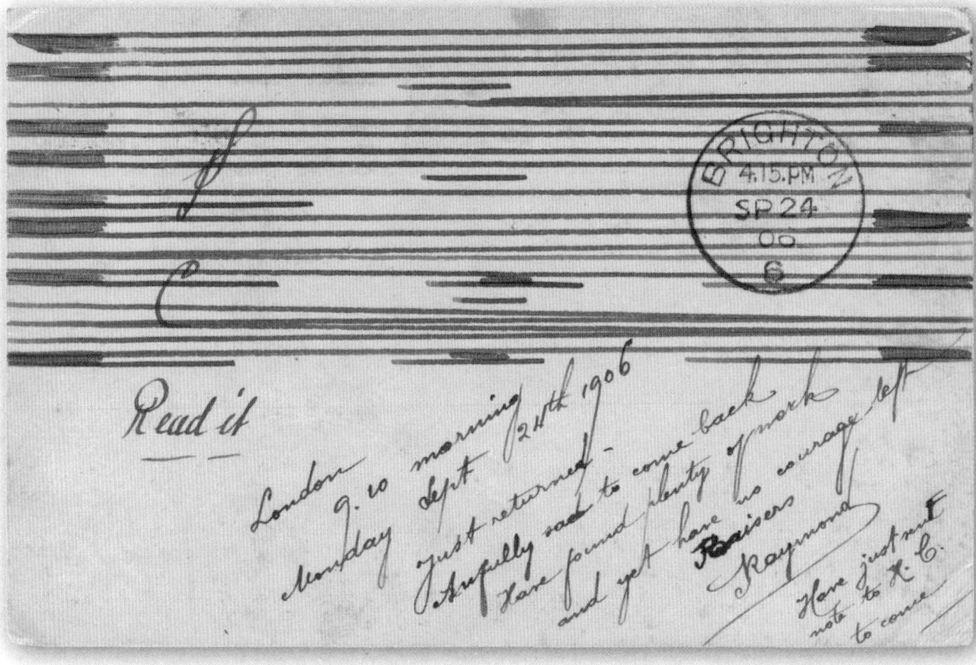

Read it

London
9.10 morning
Monday Sept 24th 1906
just returned –
Awfully sad to come back
Have found plenty of work
and yet have no courage left
Baisers
Raymond

Have just sent
note to K.C.
to come

POST CARD
LONDON
24 SEP
12-15P
1906
THIS SPACE MAY BE USED FOR PRINTED OR
WRITTEN MATTER FOR INLAND USE ONLY
E R
HALF PENNY
Miss Daisy Grimsdale
44 Egremont Place
Brighton

Corinthian Arch, Stowe, Buckingham

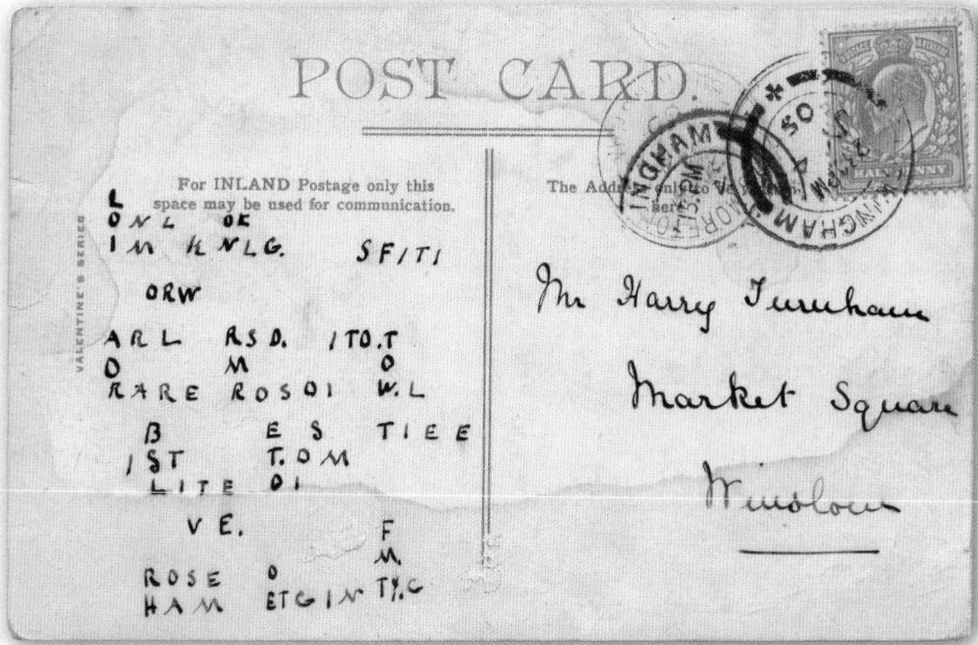
POST CARD.
VALENTINE'S SERIES
For INLAND Postage only this space may be used for communication.
The Address only to be written here.
L
ONL OK
IM KNLG. SF/TI
ORW
ARL RSD. ITO.T
O M O
RARE ROSOI W.L
B E S TIEE
IST T.OM
LITE OI
VE. F
M.
ROSE O TY.C
HAM ETGIN
Mr Harry Turnham
Market Square
Winslow

Proverbs
Be off
with the Old
Love
before you're on
with the
New.
JWS 2744

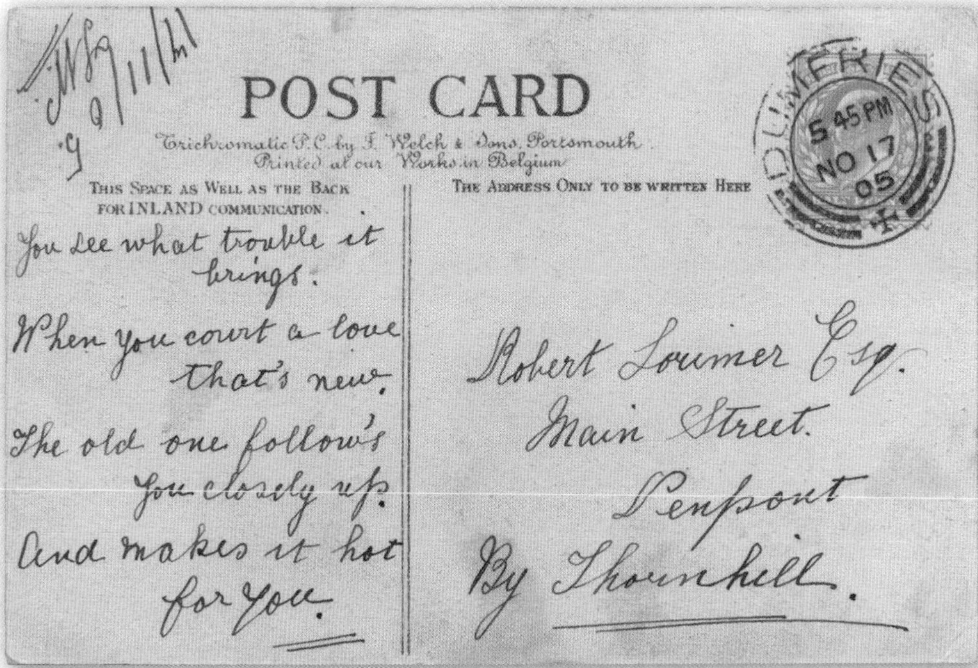
POST CARD

Trichromatic P.C. by F. Welch & Sons, Portsmouth
Printed at our Works in Belgium

THIS SPACE AS WELL AS THE BACK FOR INLAND COMMUNICATION.

THE ADDRESS ONLY TO BE WRITTEN HERE

DUMFRIES
5 45 PM
NO 17
05

You see what trouble it
brings.
When you court a love
that's new.
The old one follow's
you closely up.
And makes it hot
for you.

Robert Lorimer Esq.
Main Street.
Penpont
By Thornhill.

CLIFFORD'S INN HALL
Charles E. Flower

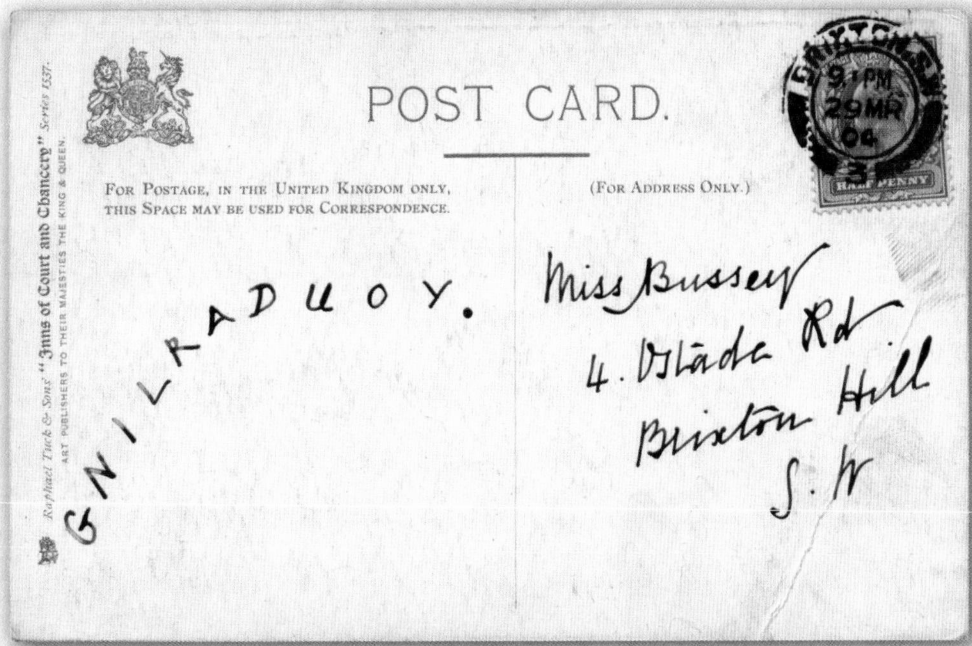
Raphael Tuck & Sons' "Inns of Court and Chancery" Series 1537.
ART PUBLISHERS TO THEIR MAJESTIES THE KING & QUEEN.
POST CARD.
FOR POSTAGE, IN THE UNITED KINGDOM ONLY, THIS SPACE MAY BE USED FOR CORRESPONDENCE.
(FOR ADDRESS ONLY.)
9 PM
29 MR
04
HALF PENNY
GNILRADUOY.
Miss Bussey
4. Ostade Rd
Brixton Hill
S.W

COPYRIGHT. S. HILDESHEIMER & Co Ltd LONDON & MANCHESTER
TOWER BRIDGE.
Have you ever seen it? Look out for it the next time you are in London
but, before then, look out for an offer that will shortly be made to you
It is bound to interest you

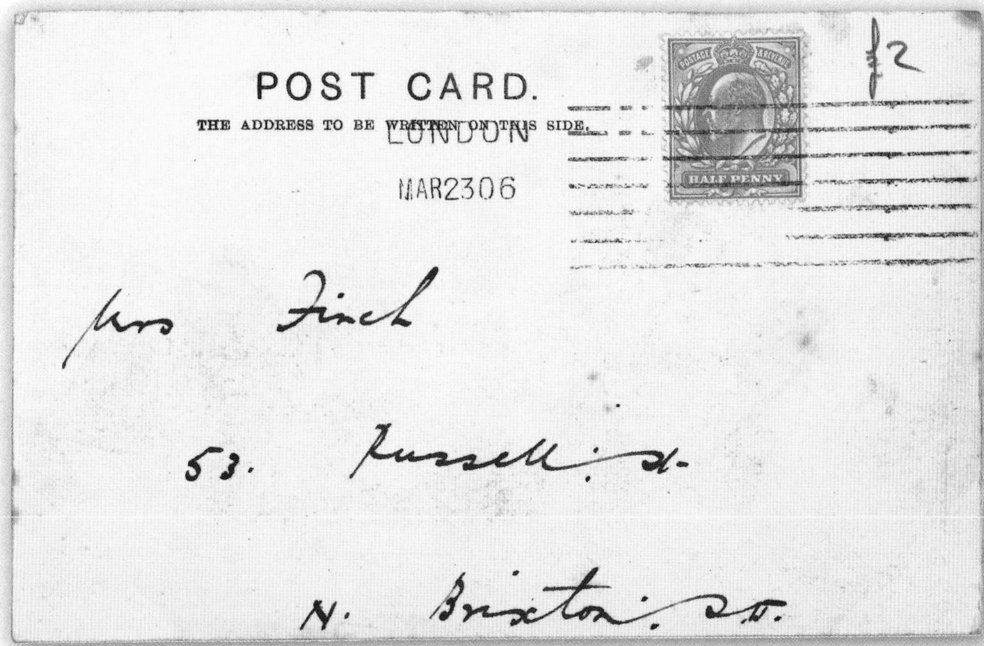
POST CARD.
THE ADDRESS TO BE WRITTEN ON THIS SIDE.
LONDON
MAR2306
POSTAGE REVENUE
HALF PENNY
Mrs Finch
53. Russell St.
N. Brixton. S.W.

Hand painted

CARTE POSTALE

LONDON, S.W. 12.15 PM SP 20 09 6

CORRESPONDANCE.

This is the latest in
picture post-cards.
Rather good isn't it?
Having splendid weather
in London.
Kind regards
A. W. Martin

ADRESSE.

Mrs A. E. Sherriff
York Villas
Anglesey Street
Hednesford
Staffs

from the Original Painting — Grand Canal. Venice — after J.M.W. Turner R.A. — in the National Gallery

Raphael Tuck & Sons' "Turner" Post Card No 53 Designed in England, Chromographed in Saxony

Sunday

No news since yesterday.
Beautiful weather for o
once but fog thick toni
wish I was at Venice or
rather wish I could pop
over for week ends. Big
case on tommorrow hope
I shall win shall be
glad when its over but
it will be the very -
exactly - if I dont win.

Am ordering season tic
et tonight which looks
healthy for summer. The rooks are setting up a fine
cawing everywhere & holding meetings on the treetop
the lambs are lumbering all over the fields the hed
ges are just going to begin to shoot & spring begin
to whisper. Soon we shall have equinoctial gales or
something unpleasant like them.
Love to the mater & all your friends GDH

POST CARD.
NOTTINGHAM
Miss Hazzledine
Hotel de Rome
Venice
ITALY

Brampton Park
Huntingdon.
Feb 21st 1904
Brampton Park
Valentines Series
Dear Janie
I thought you would like a P.C of where I am being

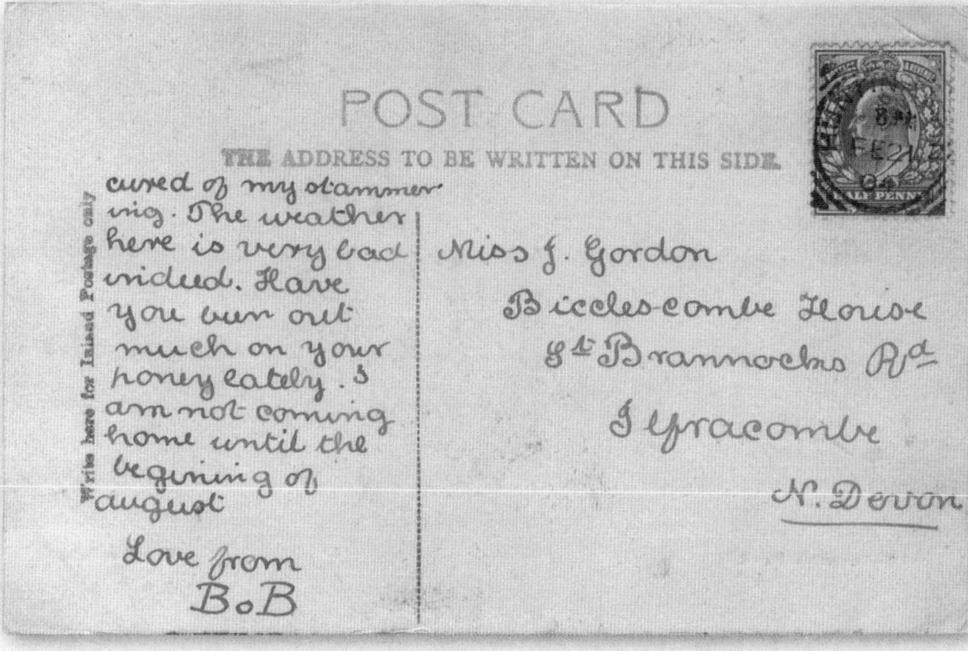

POST CARD

THE ADDRESS TO BE WRITTEN ON THIS SIDE

Write here for Inland Postage only

cured of my stammer
ing. The weather
here is very bad
indeed. Have
you been out
much on your
pony lately. I
am not coming
home until the
beginning of
august

Love from
BoB

Miss J. Gordon
Bicclescombe House
St Brannocks Rd
Ilfracombe
N. Devon

White Stone Pond, Hampstead Heath

London
£2.50 AJF

POST-CARD.

This part may be used for
Correspondence.
FOR INLAND USE ONLY.

Address only to be here.

W. H. Smith & Son, Hampstead Series 116a Finchley Rd. N. W.

0912

POSTAGE REVENUE
HALF PENNY

12.15 AM

Many thanks
for last letter.
This is the
pond on the top
of the Heath.
Great Suffragette,
Socialist, Anti-Socialist
and Salvation Army
meetings take place here
yrs A.L.F.

Miss Erica Ferguson
Fernhurst
Shrewsbury Road
Dublin

WESTMINSTER ABBEY, LONDON.

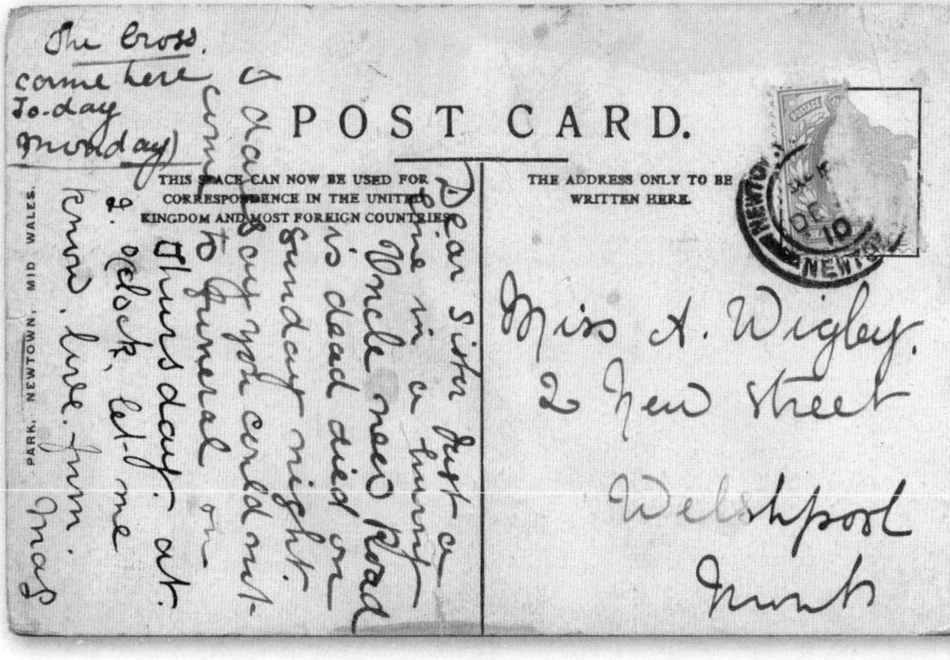
POST CARD.
THIS SPACE CAN NOW BE USED FOR CORRESPONDENCE IN THE UNITED KINGDOM AND MOST FOREIGN COUNTRIES.
THE ADDRESS ONLY TO BE WRITTEN HERE.
NEWTOWN, MID WALES.
NEWTOWN
The Cross.
come here
To-day
(Monday)
Miss A. Wigley.
2 New Street
Welshpool
Mont

31837. MANSFIELD WOODHOUSE CHURCH.

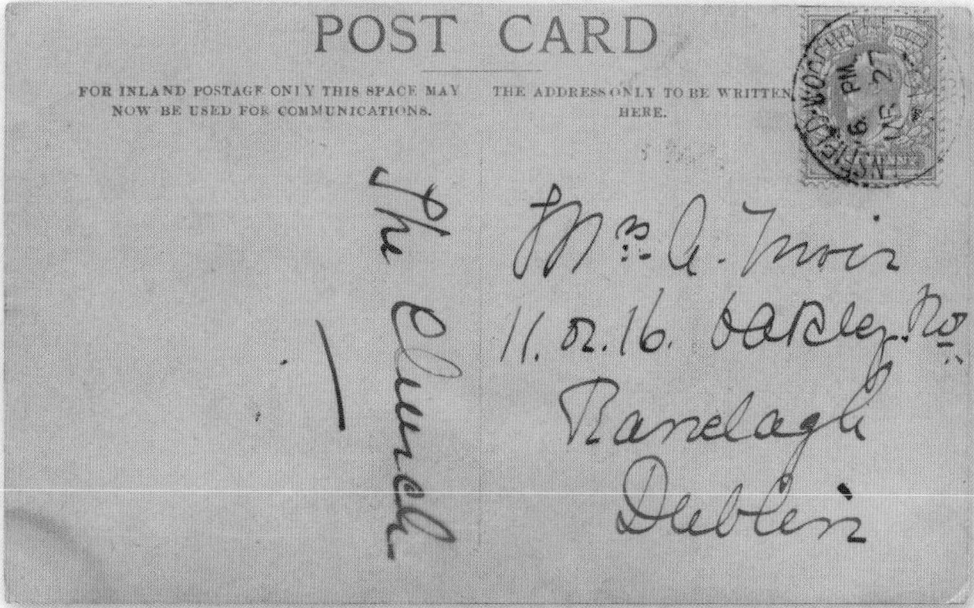
POST CARD
FOR INLAND POSTAGE ONLY THIS SPACE MAY NOW BE USED FOR COMMUNICATIONS.
THE ADDRESS ONLY TO BE WRITTEN HERE.
The Church
Ranelagh
Dublin

Pevensey Entrance to Castle.
The "Lyric" series. 109.

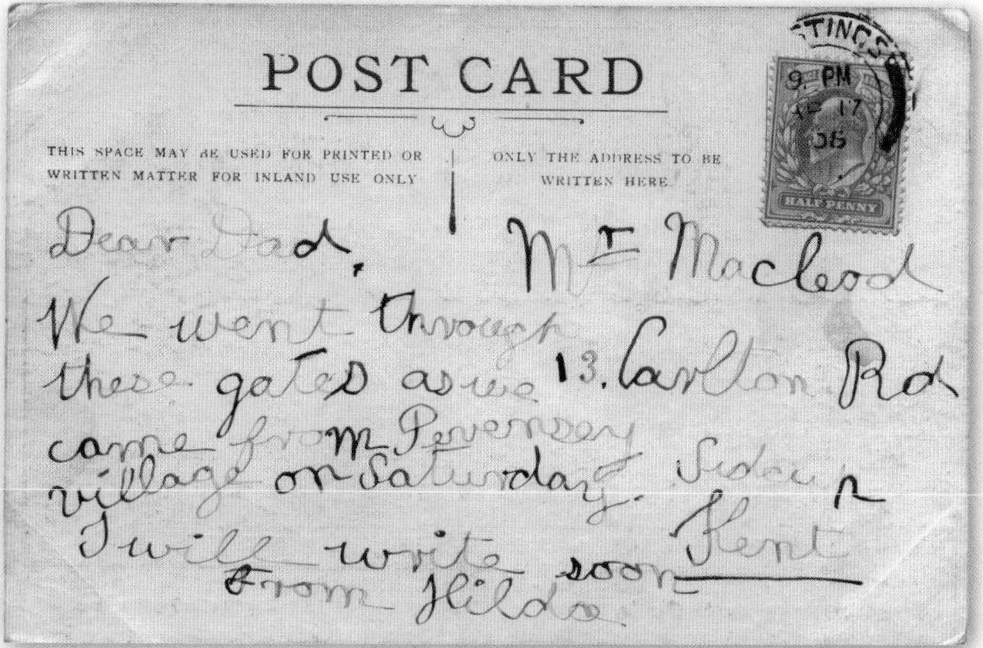

POST CARD

THIS SPACE MAY BE USED FOR PRINTED OR WRITTEN MATTER FOR INLAND USE ONLY

ONLY THE ADDRESS TO BE WRITTEN HERE.

TINGS
9 PM
17
06

HALF PENNY

Dear Dad,
We went through
these gates as we
came from Pevensey
village on Saturday.
I will write soon
From Hilda

Mr Macleod
13, Carlton Rd
Sidcup
Kent

BUDE CANAL

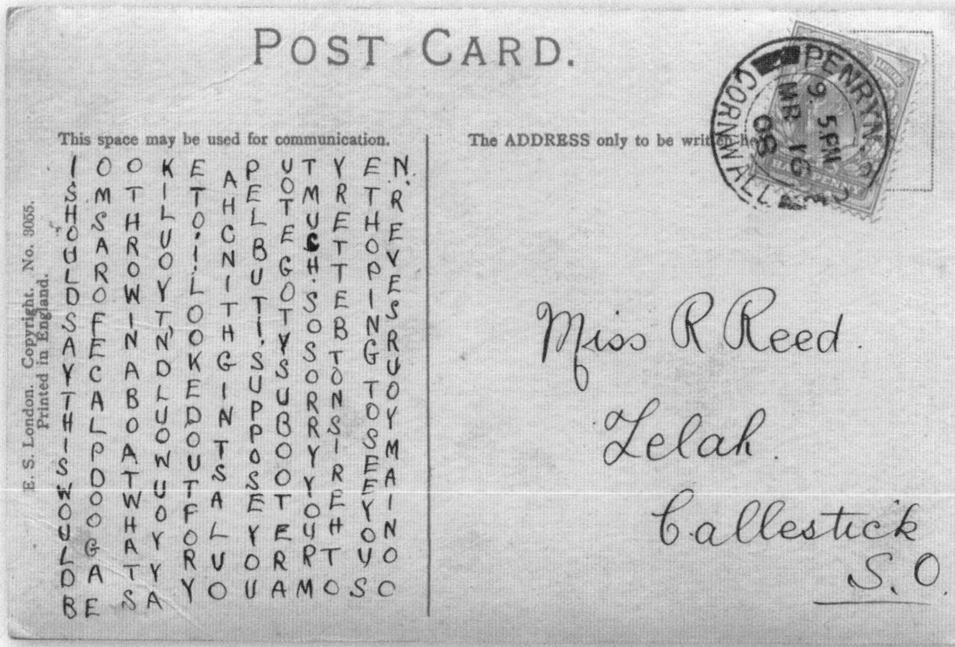

POST CARD.

PENRYN
CORNWALL
9.5 PM
MR 16
08

E. S. London. Copyright. No. 3055.
Printed in England.

This space may be used for communication.

I S H O U L D S A Y T H I S W O U L D B
E
O M S A R O F E C A L P D O O G A E
O T H R O W I N A B O A T W H A T S
K I L L U O Y T N D L U O W U O Y Y A
E T O , ! L O O K E D O U T F O R Y
A H C N I T H G I N T S A L V U O
P E L B U T I . S U P P O S E Y O U
U O T E G O T Y S U B O O T E R A
T M U C H . S O S O R R Y Y O U R M
Y R E T T E B T O N S I R E H T O
E T H O P I N G T O S E E Y O U S
N . R E V E S R U O Y M A I N O C

The ADDRESS only to be written here.

Miss R Reed.
Zelah.
Callestick
S. O.

SOUTHSEA. THE BEACH.

1962
POST CARD
FOR POSTAGE IN THE UNITED KINGDOM ONLY.
THIS SPACE MAY BE USED FOR CORRESPONDENCE.
(FOR ADDRESS ONLY)
Raphael Tuck & Sons' "Town and City" Series 2050-Portsmouth and Southsea.
ART PUBLISHERS TO THEIR MAJESTIES THE KING & QUEEN.
PHOTOTYPED IN HOLLAND
Balham
14 Apr 05.
12.15 noon today
a daughter arrived
Both doing well
Mr S A Spurgeon
13 Hunter St
Brunswick Sq
London
W.C

Market Street, Manchester.
HOPE BROTHERS
HOPE BROTHERS

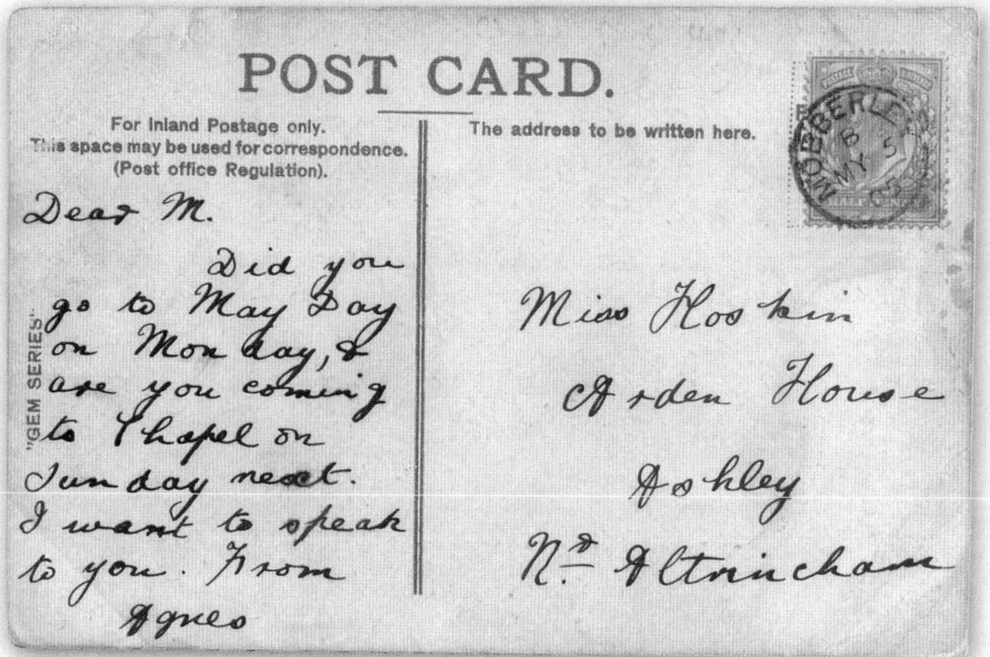

POST CARD.

For Inland Postage only.
This space may be used for correspondence.
(Post office Regulation).

"GEM SERIES"

Dear M.

Did you go to May Day on Monday, & are you coming to Chapel on Sunday next. I want to speak to you. From

Agnes

The address to be written here.

MOBBERLEY
B
MY 5
05

Miss Hoskin
Arden House
Ashley
Nr Altrincham

MR. BERTRAM WALLIS.
CLAUDE HARRIS

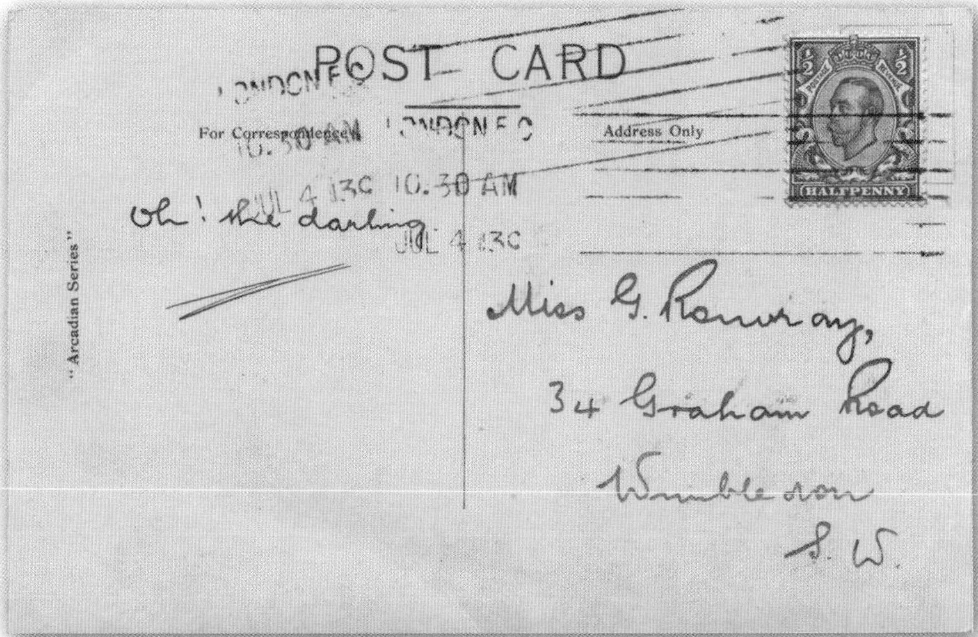
POST CARD
For Correspondence
Address Only
"Arcadian Series"
HALFPENNY
LONDON E.C
10.30 AM
Oh! the darling
34 Graham Road
Wimbledon
S.W.

1650 B
MISS RUTH VINCENT.

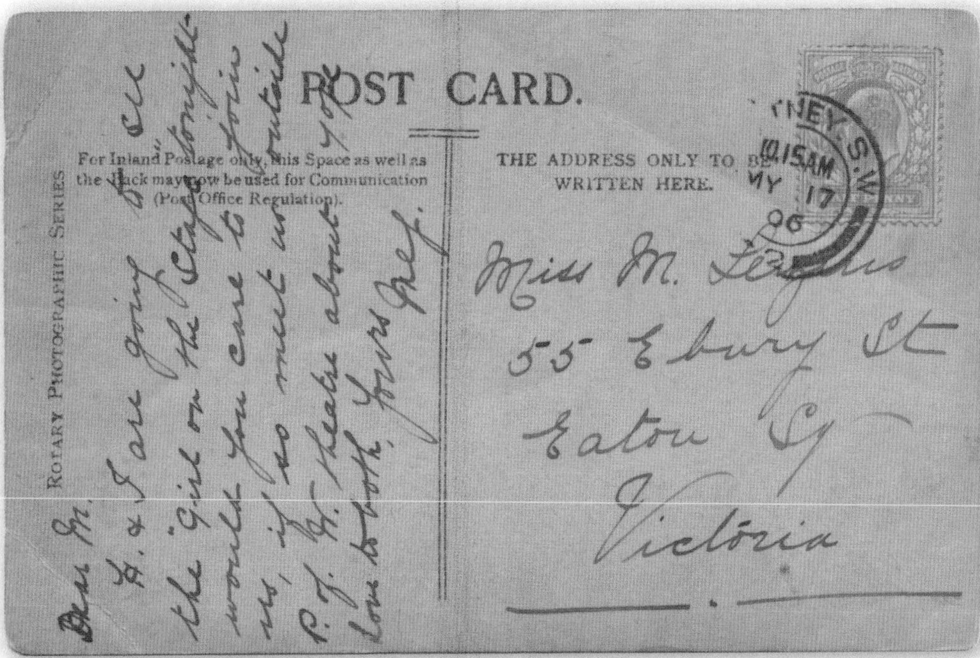
POST CARD.

For Inland Postage only, this Space as well as the Back may now be used for Communication (Post Office Regulation).

ROTARY PHOTOGRAPHIC SERIES

THE ADDRESS ONLY TO BE WRITTEN HERE.

Dear M.
F. & I are going to see
the "Girl on the Stage" tonight
would you care to join
us, if so meet us outside
P.T. [illegible] Theatre about 7.45
Love to both, Yours Meg.

Miss M. [illegible]
55 Ebury St
Eaton Sq
Victoria

R. A. M. C. MEMORIAL GUN HILL, ALDERSHOT

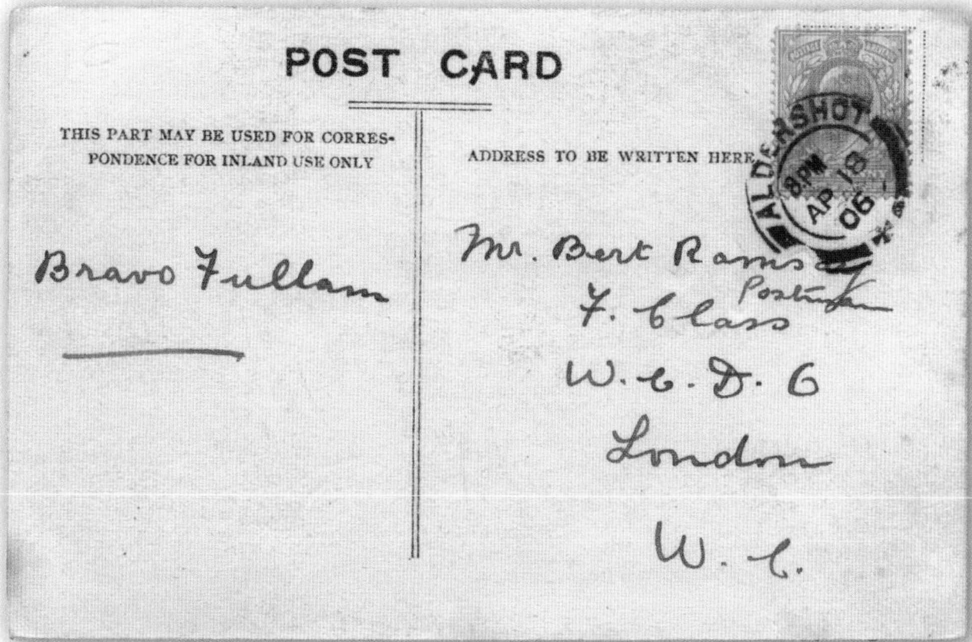
POST CARD
THIS PART MAY BE USED FOR CORRES-
PONDENCE FOR INLAND USE ONLY
ADDRESS TO BE WRITTEN HERE
ALDERSHOT
8PM
AP
06
Bravo Fullam
Mr. Bert
F. Class
W.C.D. 6
London
W.C.

New Entrance Lodge, Arundel Castle
A. W. Lapworth, The Arundel Stationery and Fancy Goods Store. a 382 | 226

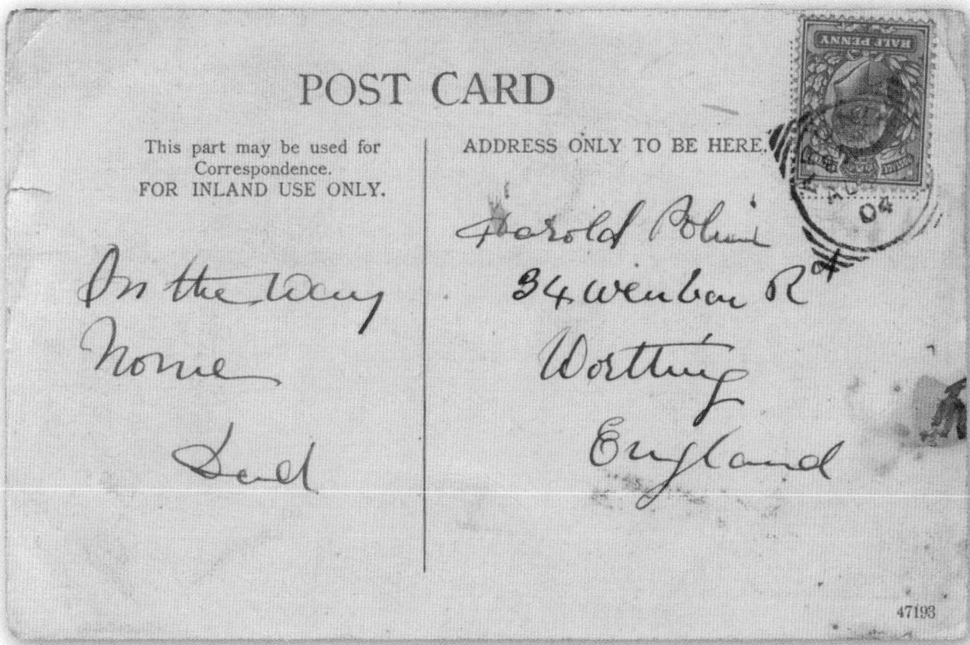

POST CARD

This part may be used for Correspondence.
FOR INLAND USE ONLY.

On the Way Home

Dad

ADDRESS ONLY TO BE HERE.

Harold Robins
34 Wenban Rd
Worthing
England

HALF PENNY

04

47193

A. W. Hayes
Tintern Abbey

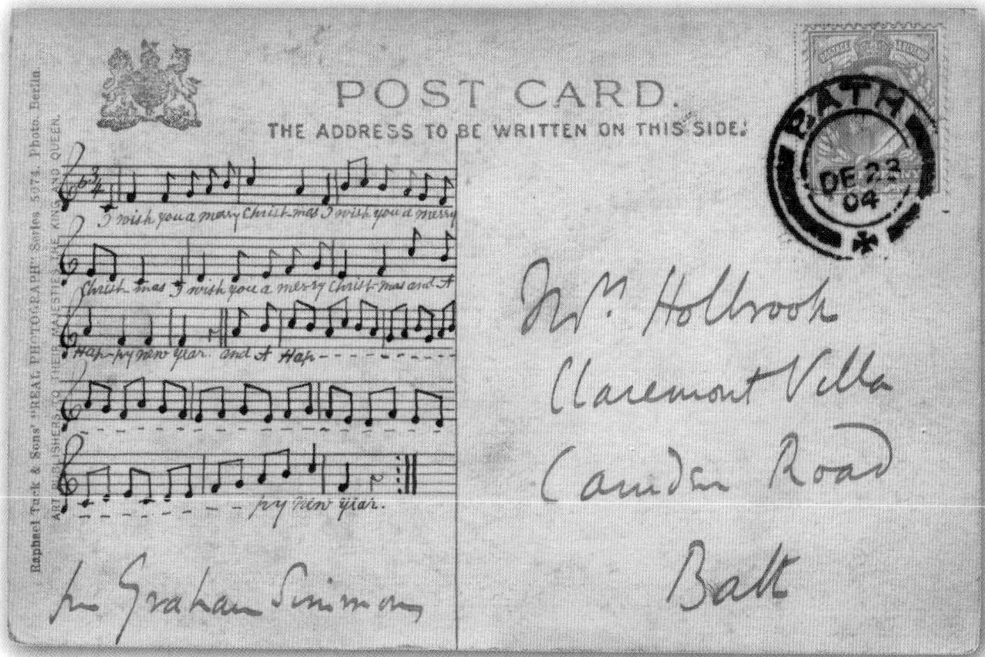
POST CARD.
THE ADDRESS TO BE WRITTEN ON THIS SIDE.
Raphael Tuck & Sons' "REAL PHOTOGRAPH" Series 5074. Photo. Berlin.
ART PUBLISHERS TO THEIR MAJESTIES THE KING AND QUEEN.
I wish you a merry Christ-mas I wish you a merry
Christ-mas I wish you a merry Christ-mas and A
Hap-py new year. and A Hap-
py new year.
BATH
DE 23
04
Claremont Villa
Camden Road
Bath

Blackpool From North Pier.

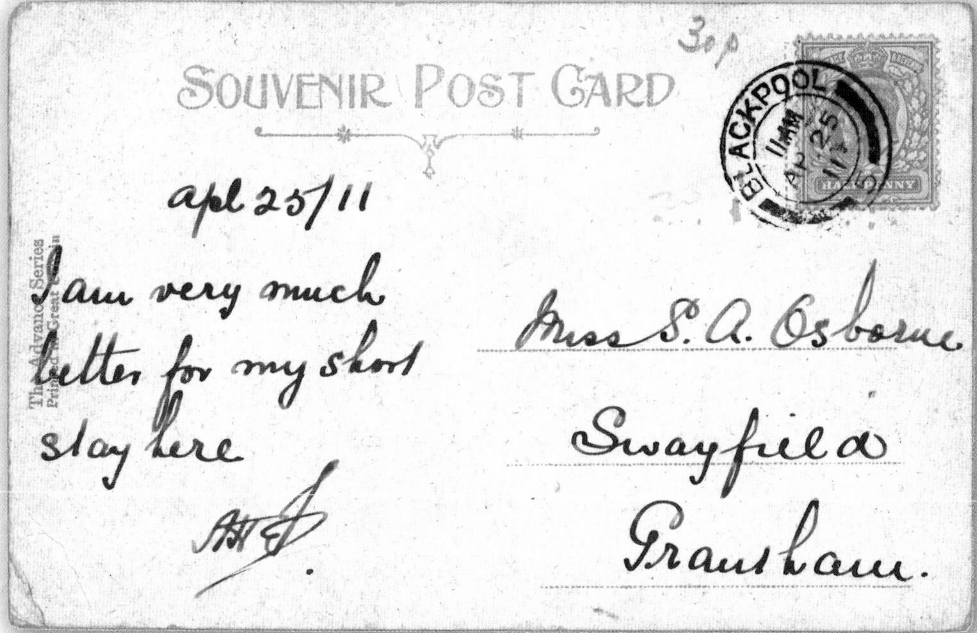

30p

SOUVENIR POST CARD

BLACKPOOL 11 AM AP 25 11

The Advance Series
Printed in Great Britain

apl 25/11

I am very much better for my short stay here

AHJ.

Miss S. A. Osborne
Swayfield
Grantham.

Raphael Tuck & Sons' "OILETTE" [Regd.] "CONNOISSEUR" Postcard 2576
WONDERFUL WHITE WINTER. From the original painting by Professor Van Hier.
ART PUBLISHERS TO THEIR MAJESTIES THE KING & QUEEN.

POST CARD.

FOR POSTAGE, IN THE UNITED KINGDOM ONLY, THIS SPACE MAY BE USED FOR CORRESPONDENCE.

In the [illegible]
[illegible] the [illegible]
[illegible]. [illegible]
I asked [illegible]
and he said it was
not he that [illegible]
Have you been talking
to [illegible] since
Monday.

Printed in England.

(FOR ADDRESS ONLY.)

DORCHESTER 10AM MR 23 05 256

Miss E. A. Wills
15 Millers Close
The Grove
Dorchester

D. F. & Co. York.
OLD MILL CREEK DARTMOUTH

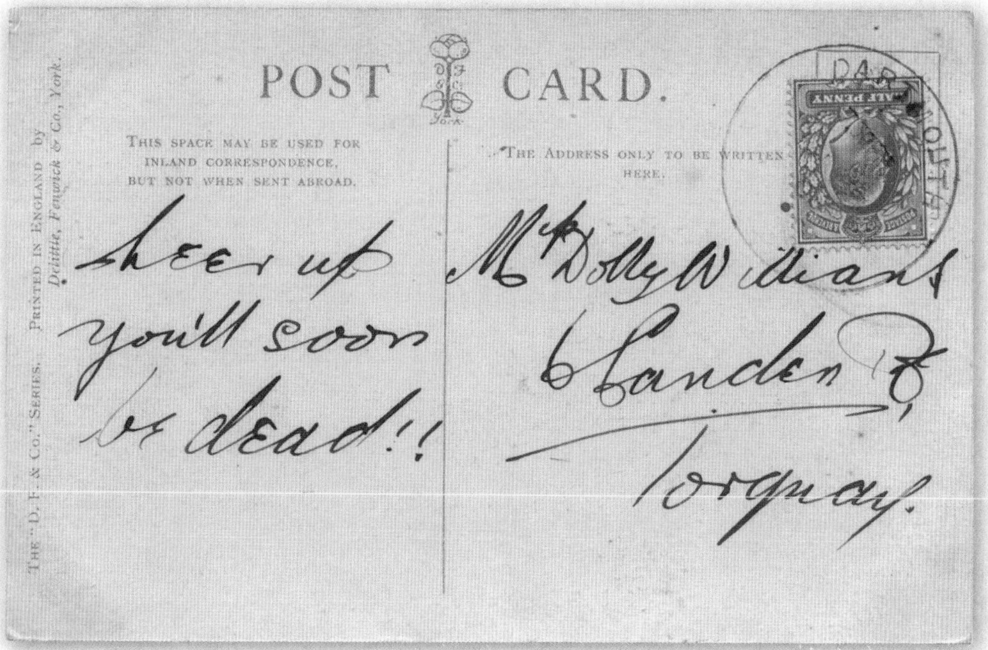
POST CARD.
THIS SPACE MAY BE USED FOR INLAND CORRESPONDENCE, BUT NOT WHEN SENT ABROAD.
THE ADDRESS ONLY TO BE WRITTEN HERE.
THE "D. F. & Co." SERIES. PRINTED IN ENGLAND by Delittle, Fenwick & Co., York.
Cheer up you'll soon be dead!!
Mrs Dolly Williams
6 Camden Rd
Torquay.

SHIRLAND ROAD. W. 30371.

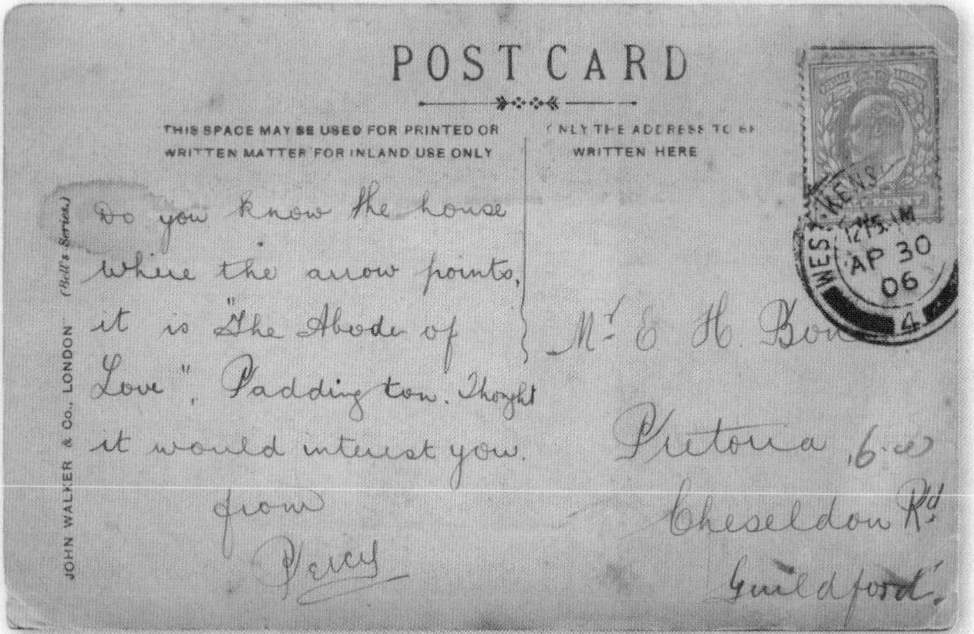

POST CARD

THIS SPACE MAY BE USED FOR PRINTED OR WRITTEN MATTER FOR INLAND USE ONLY

ONLY THE ADDRESS TO BE WRITTEN HERE

JOHN WALKER & Co., LONDON (Bell's Series.)

Do you know the house where the arrow points, it is "The Abode of Love", Paddington. Thoght it would interest you.

from

Percy

WEST KENS 12.15 AM AP 30 06 4

Mr E H Bo[...]

Pretoria, 6 ...

Cheseldon Rd

Guildford.

5101 MIDLAND STATION, DERBY.

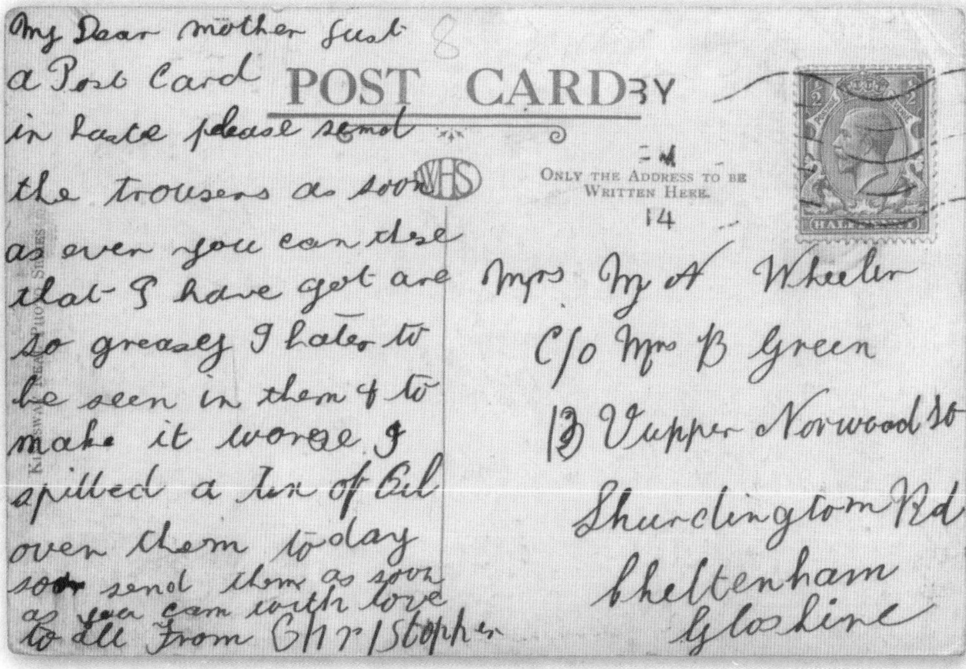

My Dear mother Just
a Post Card
in haste please send
the trousers as soon
as ever you can these
that I have got are
so greasy I hate to
be seen in them & to
make it worse I
spilled a tin of oil
over them today
soo send them as soon
as you can with love
to all From Christopher

8

POST CARD

ONLY THE ADDRESS TO BE WRITTEN HERE.

Mrs M A Wheeler
C/o Mrs B Green
13 Upper Norwood St
Shurdington Rd
Cheltenham
Glosshire

Winchester from Cathedral Tower, looking East
M.J.R., B. No.2065

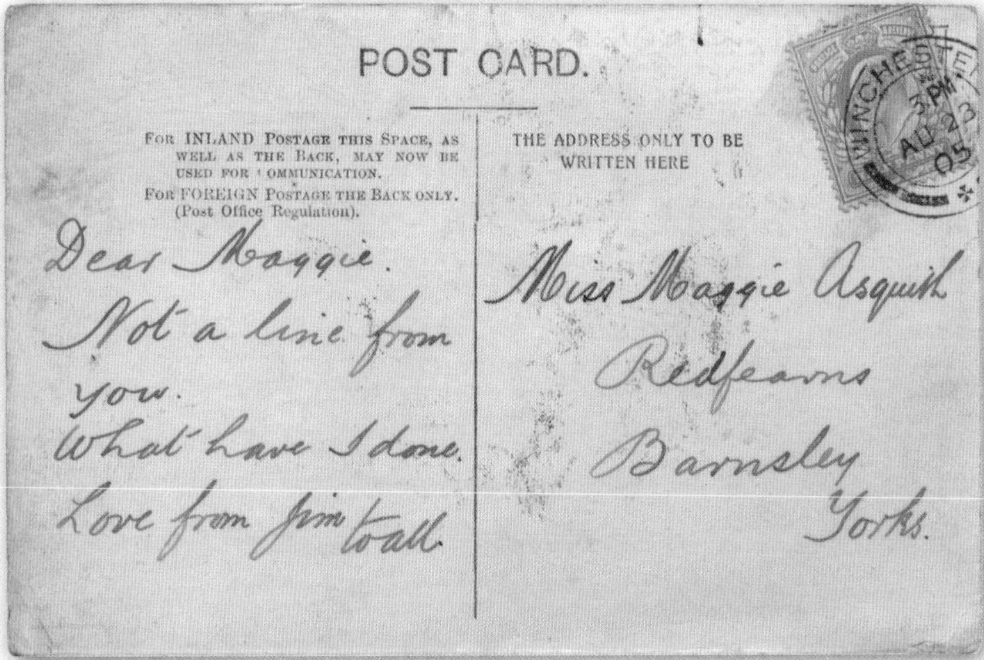
POST CARD.

FOR INLAND POSTAGE THIS SPACE, AS WELL AS THE BACK, MAY NOW BE USED FOR COMMUNICATION.
FOR FOREIGN POSTAGE THE BACK ONLY.
(Post Office Regulation).

THE ADDRESS ONLY TO BE WRITTEN HERE

WINCHESTER
3 PM
AU 23
05

Dear Maggie.
Not a line from you.
What have I done.
Love from Jim to all.

Miss Maggie Asquith
Redfearns
Barnsley
Yorks.

My word! if I catch you NAPPING!!!

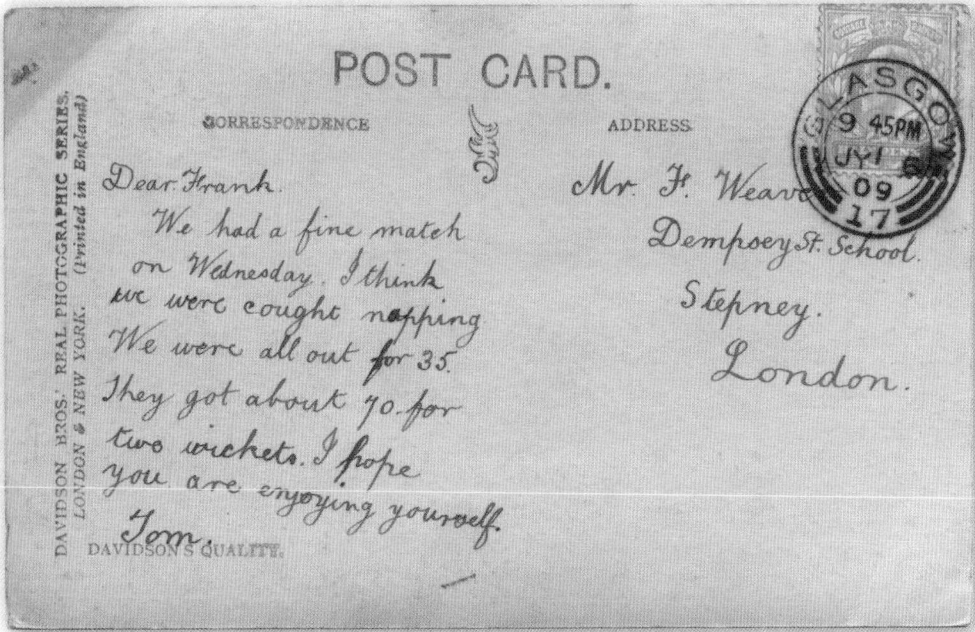

POST CARD.

CORRESPONDENCE

Dear Frank.
We had a fine match
on Wednesday. I think
we were cought napping
We were all out for 35.
They got about 70. for
two wickets. I hope
you are enjoying yourself.
Tom.

ADDRESS

Mr. F. Weave[r]
Dempsey St. School.
Stepney.
London.

GLASGOW 9 45PM JY 1 09 17

DAVIDSON BROS.' REAL PHOTOGRAPHIC SERIES.
LONDON & NEW YORK. (Printed in England)

DAVIDSON'S QUALITY.

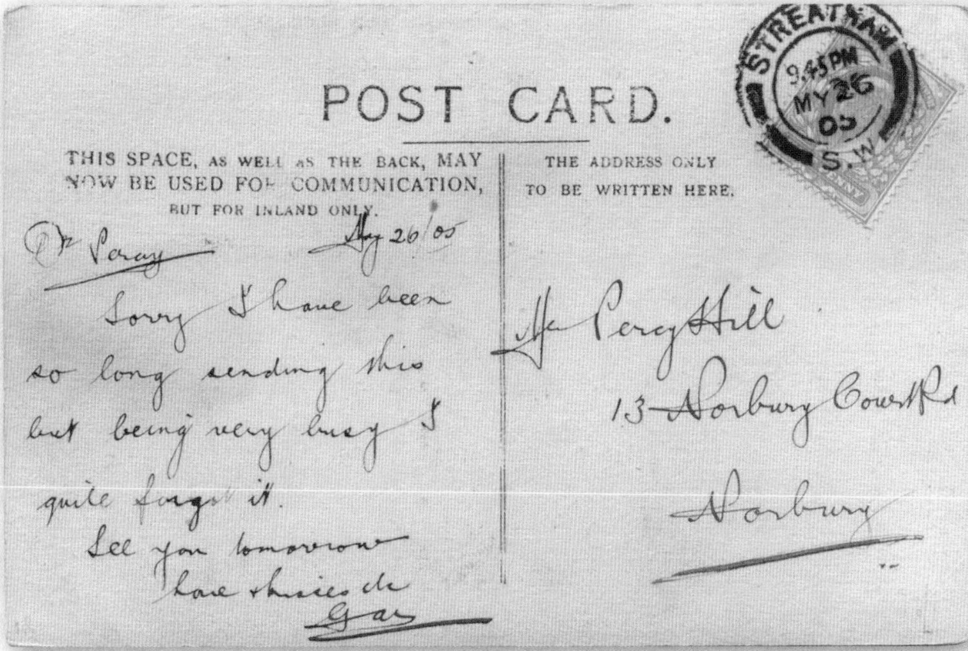
POST CARD.

THIS SPACE, AS WELL AS THE BACK, MAY NOW BE USED FOR COMMUNICATION, BUT FOR INLAND ONLY.

THE ADDRESS ONLY TO BE WRITTEN HERE.

STREATHAM 9.45 PM MY 26 05 S.W.

Dr Percy My 26/05

Sorry I have been so long sending this but being very busy I quite forgot it.

See you tomorrow

love & kisses

Gas

Mr Percy Hill
13 Norbury Court Rd
Norbury

Deer Stalking. Returning with the Spoils.

Raphael Tuck & Sons' "British Sports." Series 1409. Chromotyped in Saxony.
ART PUBLISHERS TO THEIR MAJESTIES THE KING & QUEEN.

£3

POST CARD.

FOR POSTAGE, IN THE UNITED KINGDOM ONLY, THIS SPACE MAY BE USED FOR CORRESPONDENCE.

(FOR ADDRESS ONLY).

9.15 PM
OC 30

Yours
Vernon

Miss Lowe
39 Harrow Side
South Shore

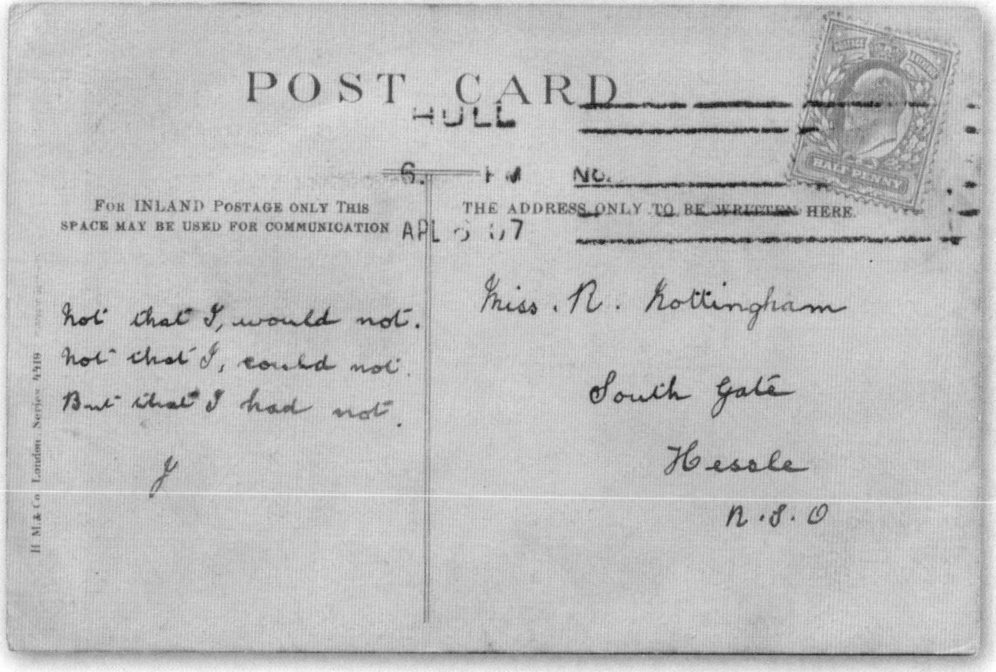
POST CARD

HULL

6. NC.

APL 07

FOR INLAND POSTAGE ONLY THIS SPACE MAY BE USED FOR COMMUNICATION

Not that I, would not.
Not that I, could not.
But that I had not.

J

THE ADDRESS ONLY TO BE WRITTEN HERE.

Miss. R. Kottingham
South Gate
Hessle
R.S.O

H M & Co London. Series 4319

Raphael Tuck & Sons' "Rembrandesque" Postcard. Series 825. Photo by Lyddell Sawyer.
THE VILLAGE BELLE

POST CARD.
THE ADDRESS TO BE WRITTEN ON THIS SIDE.
04
C/o B. Bennett
High St
Dunstable

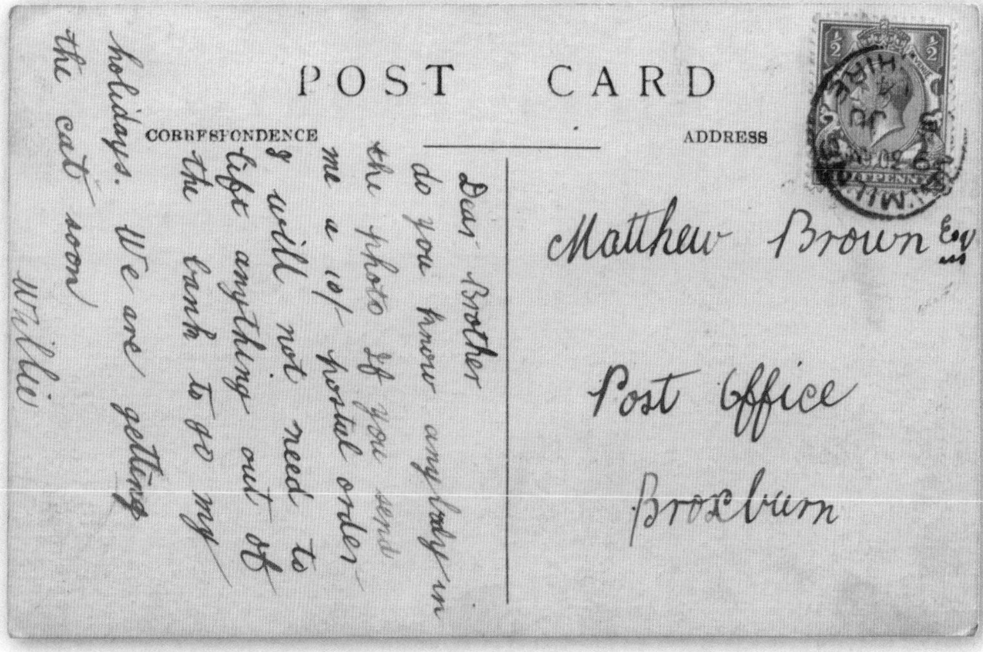

POST CARD

CORRESPONDENCE

Dear Brother
do you know anybody in
the photo If you send
me a 10/- postal order
I will not need to
lift anything out of
the bank to go my
holidays. We are getting
the cat soon
Willie

ADDRESS

Matthew Brown Esq
Post Office
Broxburn

ON GUARD.

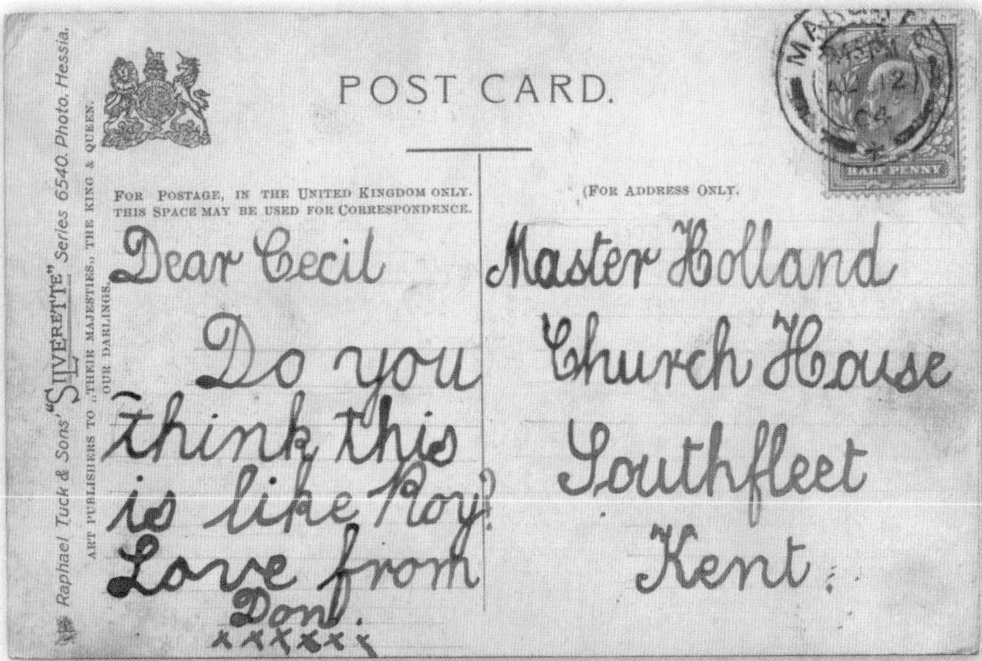
POST CARD.

FOR POSTAGE, IN THE UNITED KINGDOM ONLY.
THIS SPACE MAY BE USED FOR CORRESPONDENCE.

Dear Cecil
Do you
think this
is like Roy?
Love from
Don.
xxxxxx

(FOR ADDRESS ONLY.

Master Holland
Church House
Southfleet
Kent.

HALF PENNY

Raphael Tuck & Sons' "SILVERETTE" Series 6540. Photo. Hessia.
ART PUBLISHERS TO THEIR MAJESTIES, THE KING & QUEEN.
OUR DARLINGS.

1907
Donald

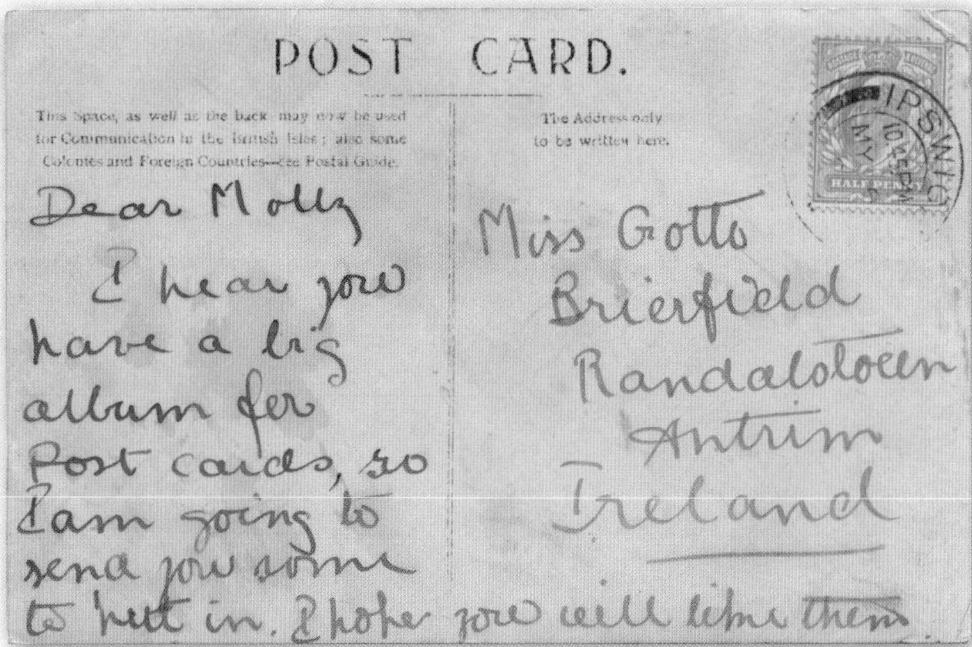

POST CARD.

This Space, as well as the back may now be used for Communication in the British Isles; also some Colonies and Foreign Countries—See Postal Guide.

The Address only to be written here.

Dear Molly

I hear you have a big album for Post cards, so I am going to send you some to put in. I hope you will like them.

Miss Gotto
Brierfield
Randalstown
Antrim
Ireland

The Dingle Colwyn Bay.

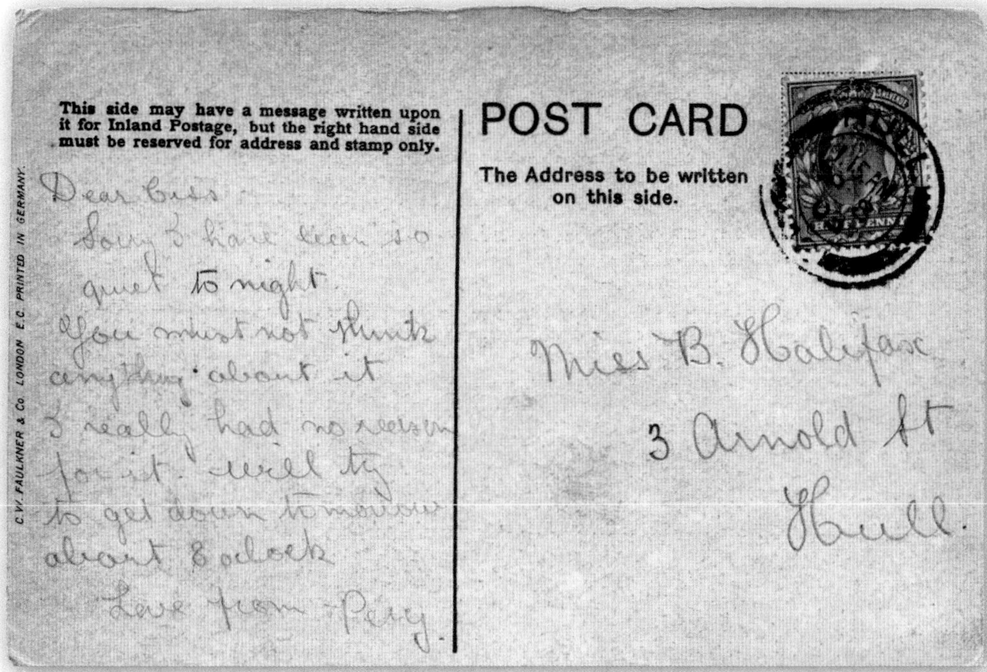
This side may have a message written upon it for Inland Postage, but the right hand side must be reserved for address and stamp only.
C.W. FAULKNER & Co. LONDON E.C. PRINTED IN GERMANY.
Dear Bess
Sorry I have been so
quiet to night
You must not think
anything about it
I really had no reason
for it. will try
to get down tomorrow
about 8 o'clock
Love from Percy.
POST CARD
The Address to be written on this side.
HALFPENNY
Miss B. Halifax
3 Arnold St
Hull.

St. Sepulchre Gate, Doncaster
Valentines Series

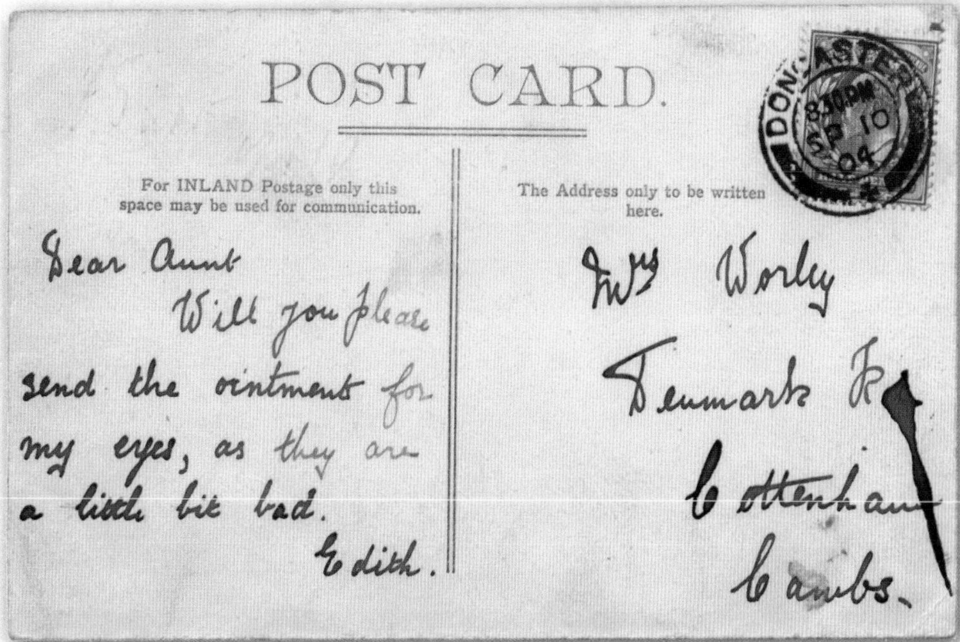
POST CARD.

DONCASTER
8.30 PM
SP 10
04

For INLAND Postage only this space may be used for communication.

Dear Aunt
Will you please
send the ointment for
my eyes, as they are
a little bit bad.
Edith.

The Address only to be written here.

Mrs Worley
Denmark Rd
Cottenham
Cambs.

WHITE HOUSE, BLACKSTONE EDGE

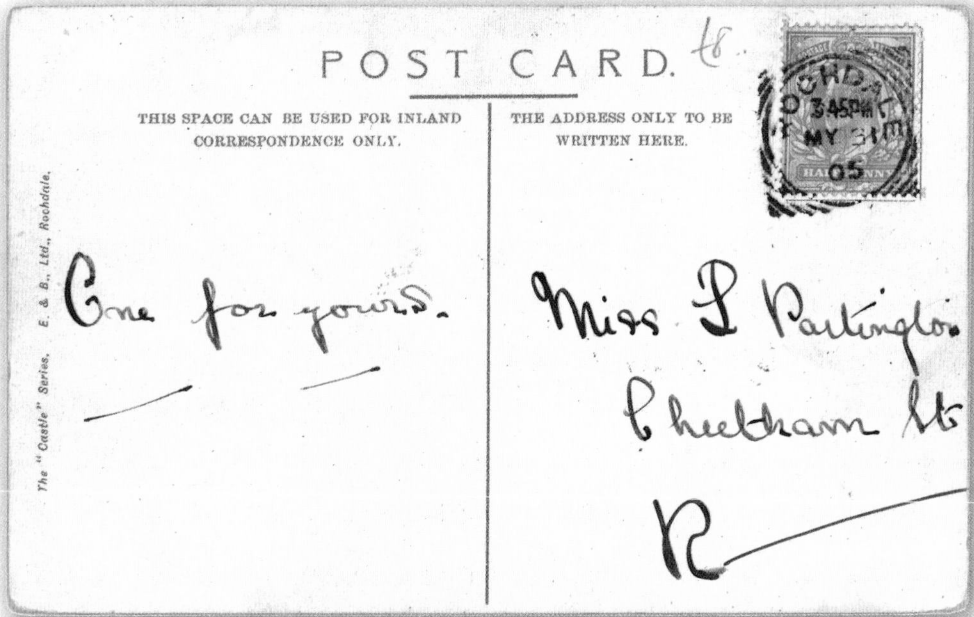

POST CARD.

THIS SPACE CAN BE USED FOR INLAND CORRESPONDENCE ONLY.

THE ADDRESS ONLY TO BE WRITTEN HERE.

The "Castle" Series. E. & B., Ltd., Rochdale.

ROCHDALE 3.45PM MY 31 05

One for yours.

Miss L Partington
Cheetham St
R

669.T (MATT)
G 669.T (GLOSSY)
MR. LEWIS WALLER

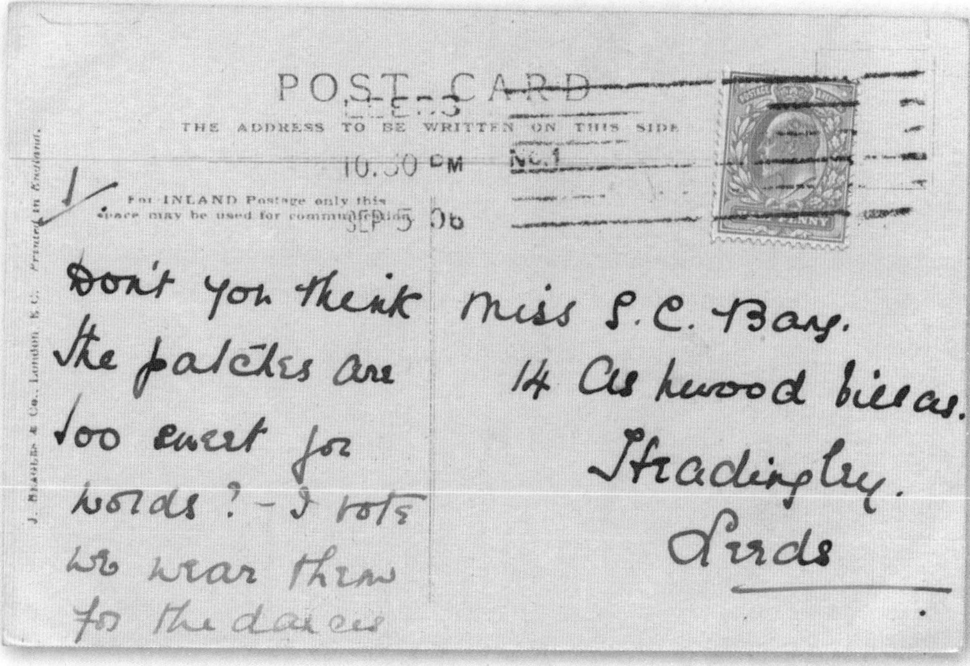

POST CARD

THE ADDRESS TO BE WRITTEN ON THIS SIDE

For INLAND Postage only this space may be used for communication.

LEEDS
10.30 PM No. 1
SEP 5 06

J. Beagles & Co., London, E.C. Printed in England.

1/

Don't you think
the patches are
too sweet for
words? - I vote
we wear them
for the dances

Miss S. C. Barr.
14 Ashwood Terrace.
Headingley.
Leeds

Love from Hilda
LEWIS WALLER

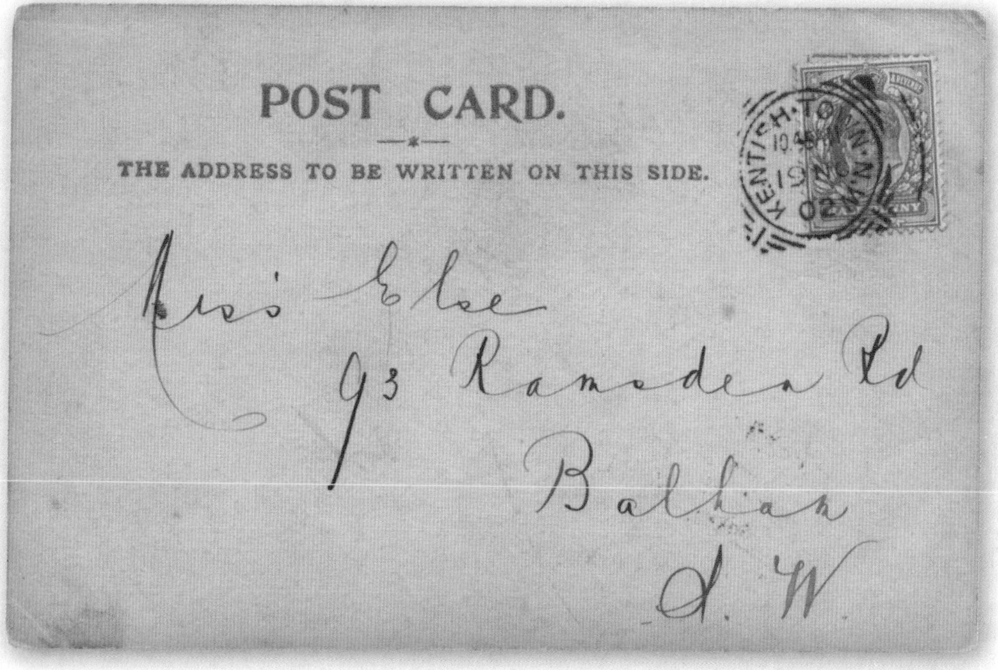
POST CARD.
THE ADDRESS TO BE WRITTEN ON THIS SIDE.
KENTISH·TOWN·N.W.
Miss Else
93 Ramsden Rd
Balham
S.W.

Whalley, King Street.

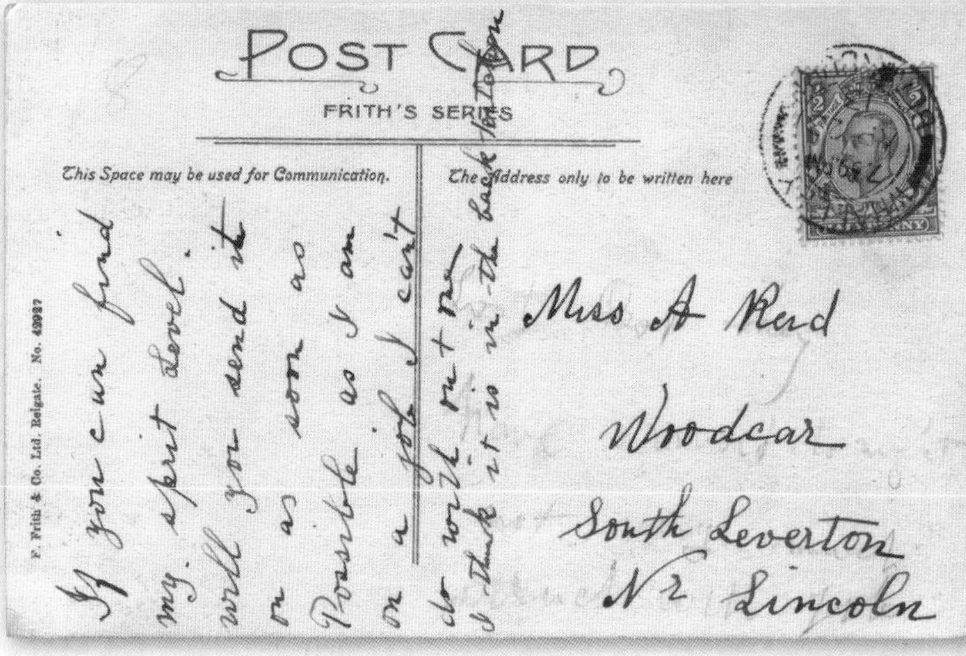

POST CARD

FRITH'S SERIES

This Space may be used for Communication.

If you can find my spirit level. will you send it me as soon as possible as I am on a job I can't do without it I think it is in the back bottom

F. Frith & Co. Ltd. Reigate. No. 42987

The Address only to be written here

Miss A Reed
Woodcar
South Leverton
Nr Lincoln

MOUNT PLEASANT INN AND TEA GARDENS.

J. F. HAMMETT, Proprietor. Note Postal Address—DAWLISH WARREN, STARCROSS.

POST CARD.

This space may be used for printed or written matter for Inland use only.

Have you heard the
result of the exams
Don't be frightened
to tell me I have
failed.
love
Connie

Only the Address to be written here.

HALF PENNY

Mrs H. G. Potts
Amonthieus
Rickmansworth
Herts

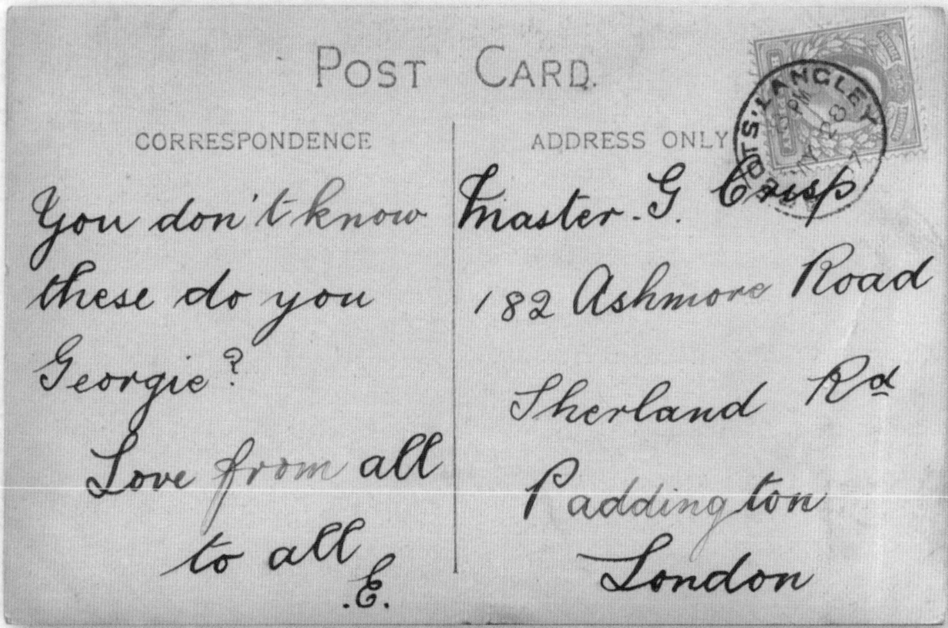
POST CARD.
CORRESPONDENCE
ADDRESS ONLY
LANGLEY
You don't know these do you Georgie?
Love from all to all
E.
Master G. Crisp
182 Ashmore Road
Sherland Rd
Paddington
London

Old Houses, Holborn — London

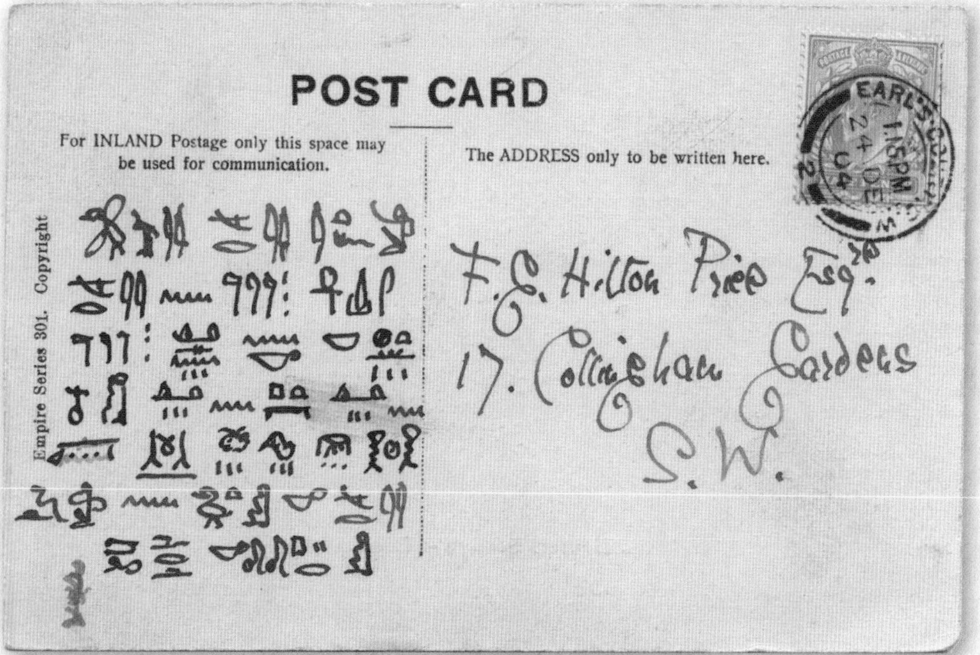
POST CARD
For INLAND Postage only this space may be used for communication.
The ADDRESS only to be written here.
Empire Series 301. Copyright
F. G. Hilton Price Esq.
17. Collingham Gardens
S.W.

SERIES 675.
ROUGH SEA OFF THE GREAT ORME, LLANDUDNO.
RAPHAEL TUCK & SONS "CONNOISSEUR" ROUGH SEA POSTCARD

POST CARD.
THE ADDRESS TO BE WRITTEN ON THIS SIDE.
Raphael Tuck & Sons' "Connoisseur" Rough Sea Post Card
Llandudno Series 676.
HALF PENNY

Eastbourne
Beachy Head
The Wrench Series No. 9772

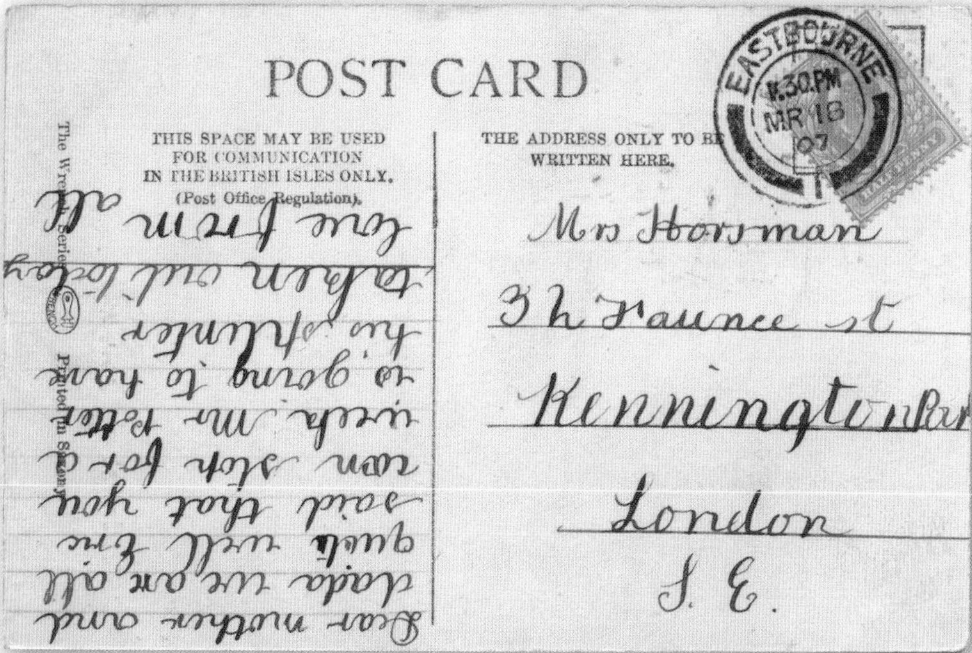
POST CARD

EASTBOURNE 4.30 PM MR 18 07

The Wrench Series. Printed in Saxony

THIS SPACE MAY BE USED FOR COMMUNICATION IN THE BRITISH ISLES ONLY. (Post Office Regulation).

Dear mother and dada we are all quite well Eric said that you can stop for a week Mr Potter is going to have his splinter taken out today love from all

THE ADDRESS ONLY TO BE WRITTEN HERE.

Mrs Horsman
34 Faunce st
Kennington Par
London
S.E.

5182-4
The Tower Bridge.
London.

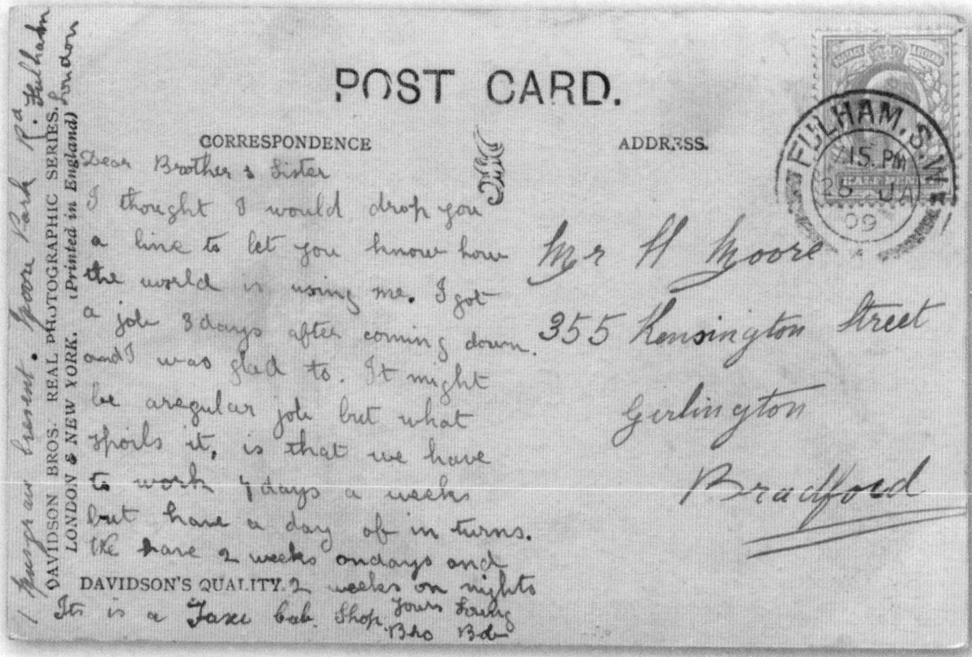
1 Musgrave Crescent. Grove Park Rd. Fulham London
DAVIDSON BROS.' REAL PHOTOGRAPHIC SERIES.
LONDON & NEW YORK. (Printed in England)

POST CARD.

CORRESPONDENCE

Dear Brother & Sister
I thought I would drop you
a line to let you know how
the world is using me. I got
a job 3 days after coming down
and I was glad to. It might
be aregular job but what
spoils it, is that we have
to work 7 days a week
but have a day of in turns.
We have 2 weeks ondays and
2 weeks on nights
It is a Taxi Cab Shop. Yours Loving
Bro Bd

DAVIDSON'S QUALITY.

ADDRESS.

FULHAM. S.W.
7.15 PM
25 JA
09

Mr H Moore
355 Kensington Street
Girlington
Bradford

LONDON. OLD HOUSES. HIGH HOLBORN.
Suppose we shall see you next week J

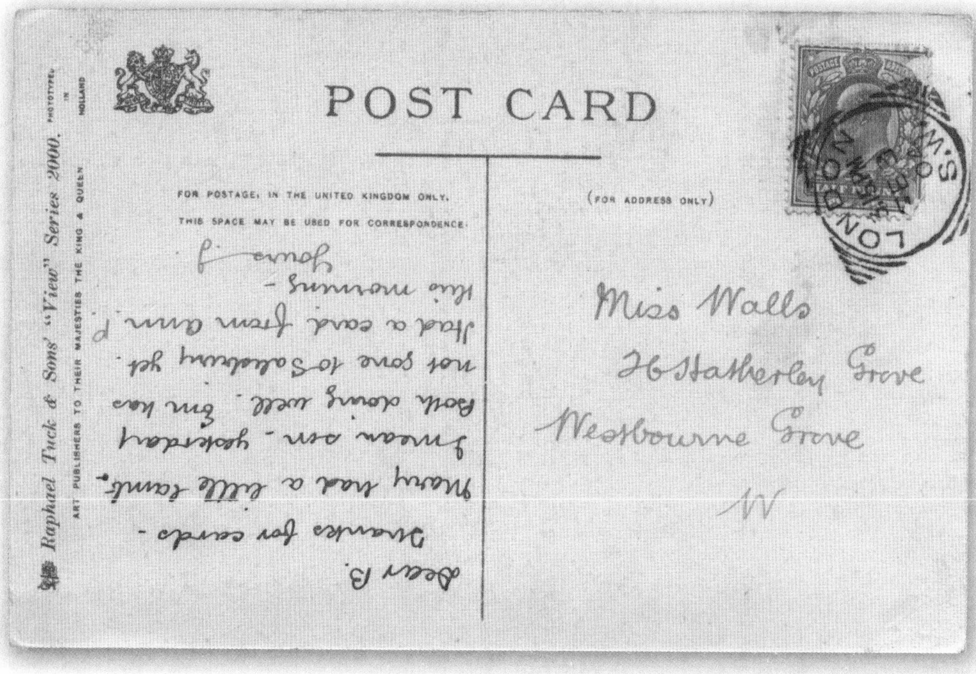
Raphael Tuck & Sons' "View" Series 2000.
ART PUBLISHERS TO THEIR MAJESTIES THE KING & QUEEN
PHOTOTYPE IN HOLLAND
POST CARD
FOR POSTAGE: IN THE UNITED KINGDOM ONLY.
THIS SPACE MAY BE USED FOR CORRESPONDENCE.
(FOR ADDRESS ONLY)
LONDON
Miss Walls
Hatherley Grove
Westbourne Grove
W

MISS GRACE LANE.
1563 E Rotary Photo. E.C.
Langfier, Glasgow.

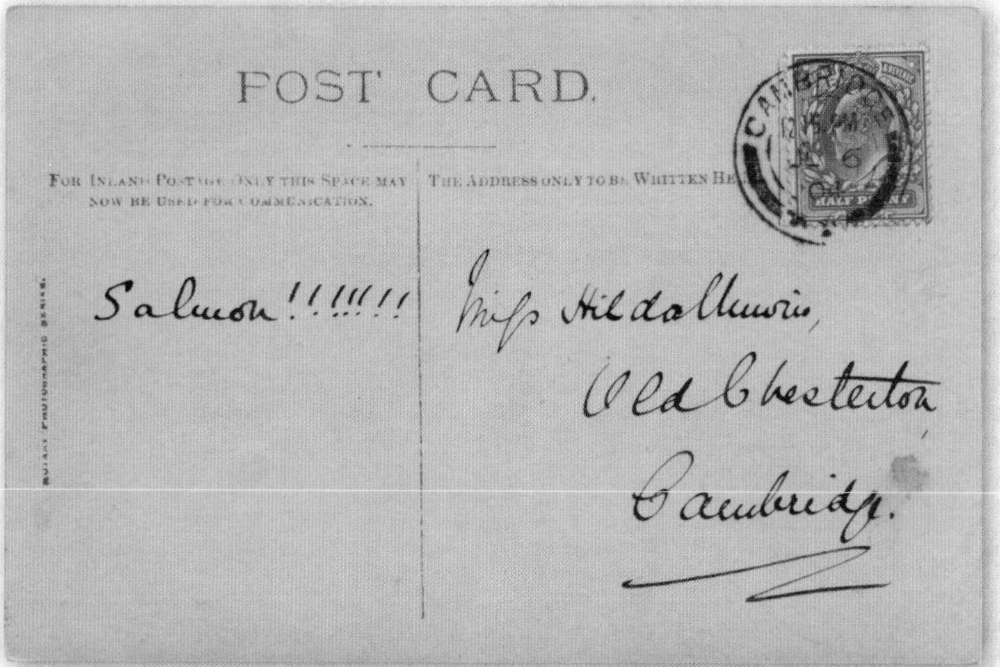
POST CARD.
FOR INLAND POSTAGE ONLY THIS SPACE MAY NOW BE USED FOR COMMUNICATION.
THE ADDRESS ONLY TO BE WRITTEN HERE
CAMBRIDGE
HALF PENNY
Salmon!!!!!!!
Old Chesterton,
Cambridge.

THE CASTLE. NOTTINGHAM.

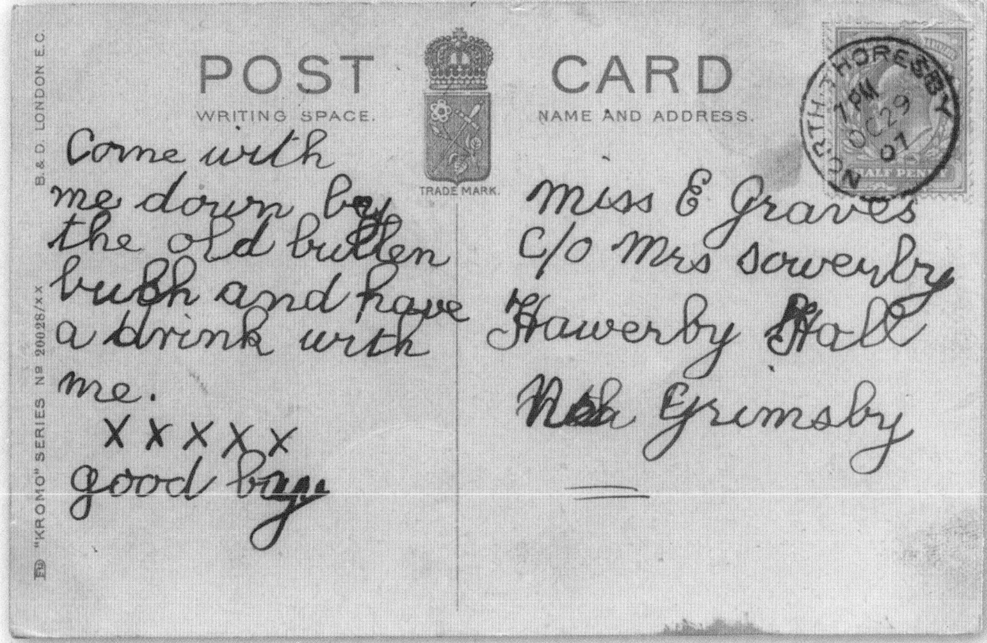
B.&D. LONDON E.C.
POST
WRITING SPACE.
TRADE MARK.
CARD
NAME AND ADDRESS.
HORESBY
7 PM
OC 29
07
HALF PENNY
Come with
me down by
the old bullen
bubh and have
a drink with
me.
xxxxx
good bye
Miss E Graves
C/o Mrs Sowerby
Hawerby Hall
Grimsby
"KROMO" SERIES № 20028/XX

366 LOCKWOOD VIADUCTS.

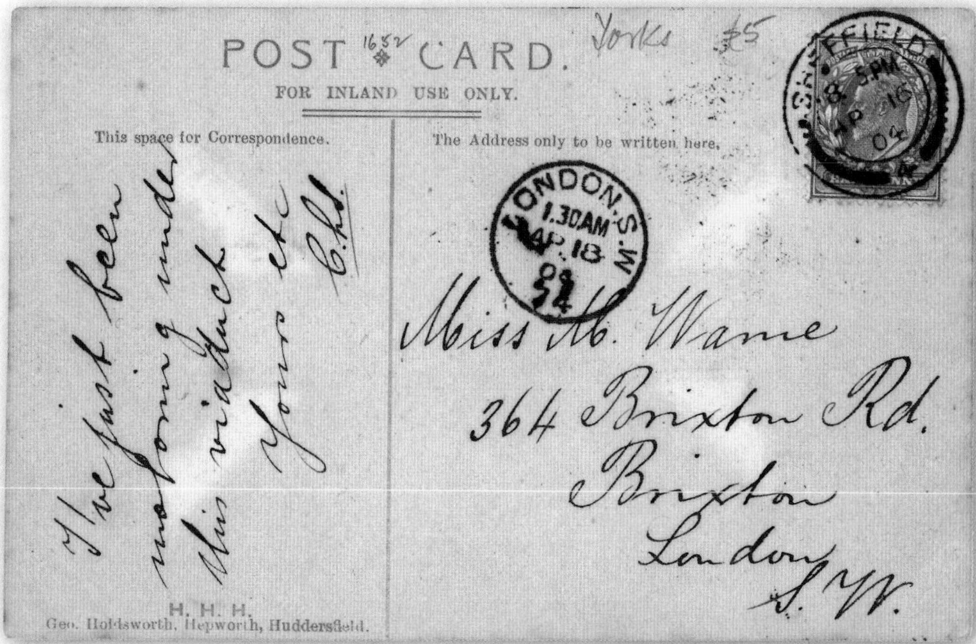
POST CARD.
FOR INLAND USE ONLY.
This space for Correspondence.
The Address only to be written here.
Yorks
SHEFFIELD
LONDON.S.W.
1.30AM
I've just been
motoring under
this viaduct
Yours etc
Miss M. Warne
364 Brixton Rd.
Brixton
London
S.W.
H. H. H.
Geo. Holdsworth, Hepworth, Huddersfield.

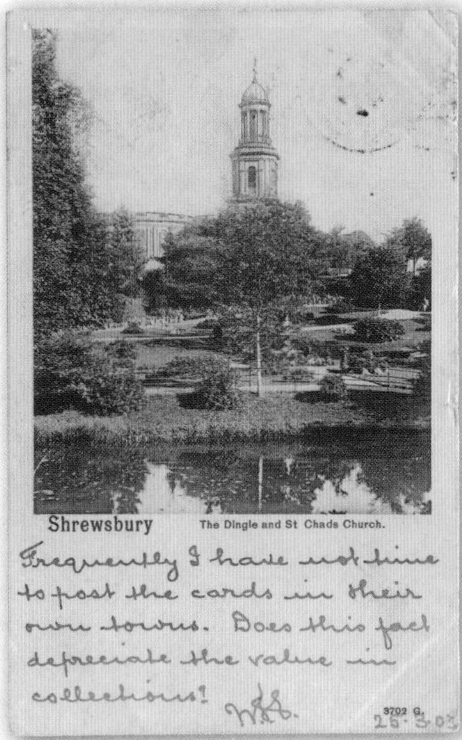
Shrewsbury
The Dingle and St Chads Church.
Frequently I have not time to post the cards in their own towns. Does this fact depreciate the value in collections?
3702 G.
25·3·03

PEACOCK BRAND

POST CARD.

TRADE MARK

THE ADDRESS TO BE WRITTEN ON THIS SIDE.

COVENTRY 4.45PM AP 27 03

PRNITED AT THE WORKS IN HAMB

Miss May Newman

Corlannan

Grove Park Road

Weston-super-Mare

Miss Marie Dainton.

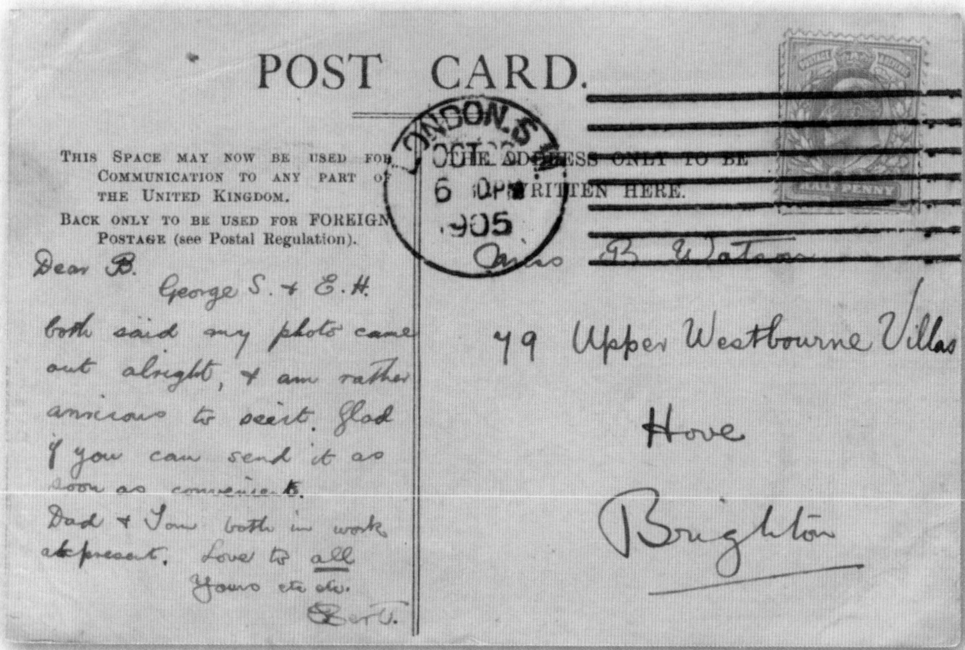
POST CARD.
THIS SPACE MAY NOW BE USED FOR COMMUNICATION TO ANY PART OF THE UNITED KINGDOM.
BACK ONLY TO BE USED FOR FOREIGN POSTAGE (see Postal Regulation).
THE ADDRESS ONLY TO BE WRITTEN HERE.
LONDON.S.W.
OCT
6 PM
1905
HALFPENNY
Dear B.
George S. & E.H.
both said my photo came out alright, & am rather anxious to see it. Glad if you can send it as soon as convenient.
Dad & Tom both in work at present. Love to all
Yours etc etc.
Bert.
Miss B. Watson
49 Upper Westbourne Villas
Hove
Brighton

THE
Is THIS BLISS?

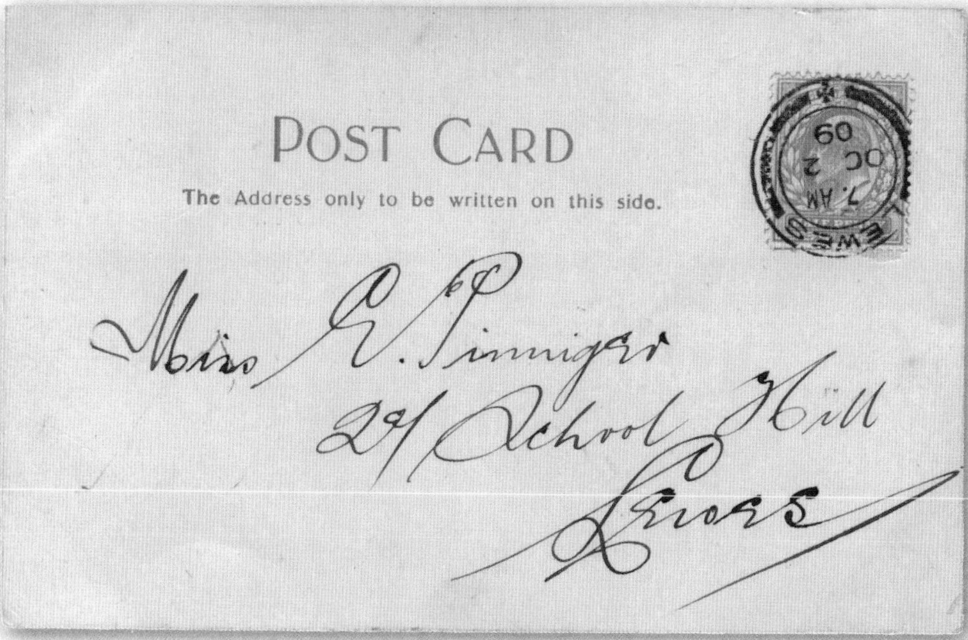
POST CARD
The Address only to be written on this side.
Miss E. Pinniger
29 School Hill
Lewes

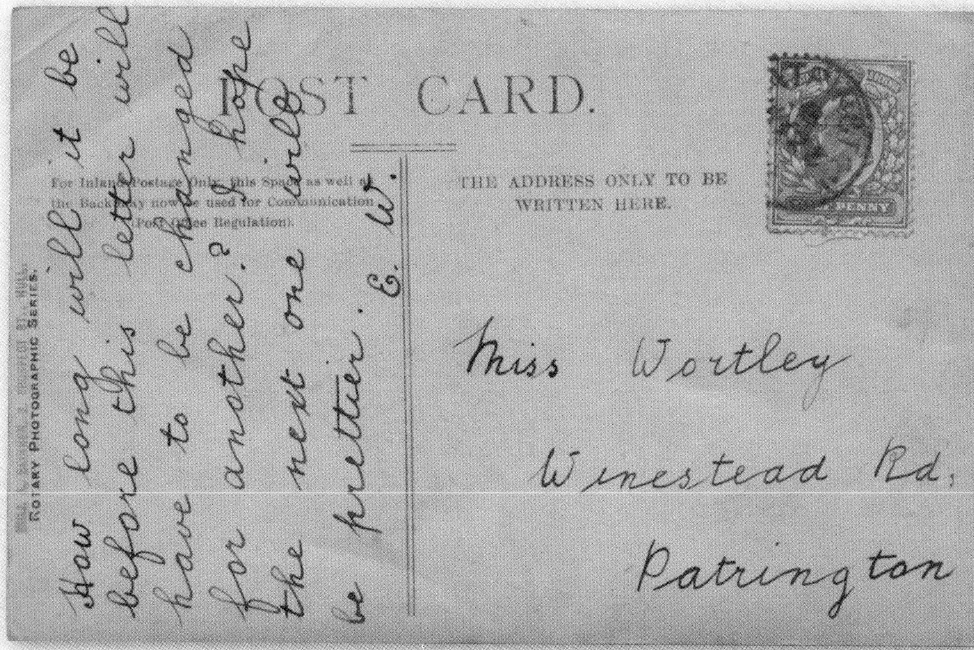

POST CARD.

For Inland Postage Only, this Space as well as the Back may now be used for Communication (Post Office Regulation).

ROTARY PHOTOGRAPHIC SERIES.

How long will it be before this letter will have to be changed for another? I hope the next one will be prettier. E. W.

THE ADDRESS ONLY TO BE WRITTEN HERE.

Miss Wortley
Winestead Rd,
Patrington

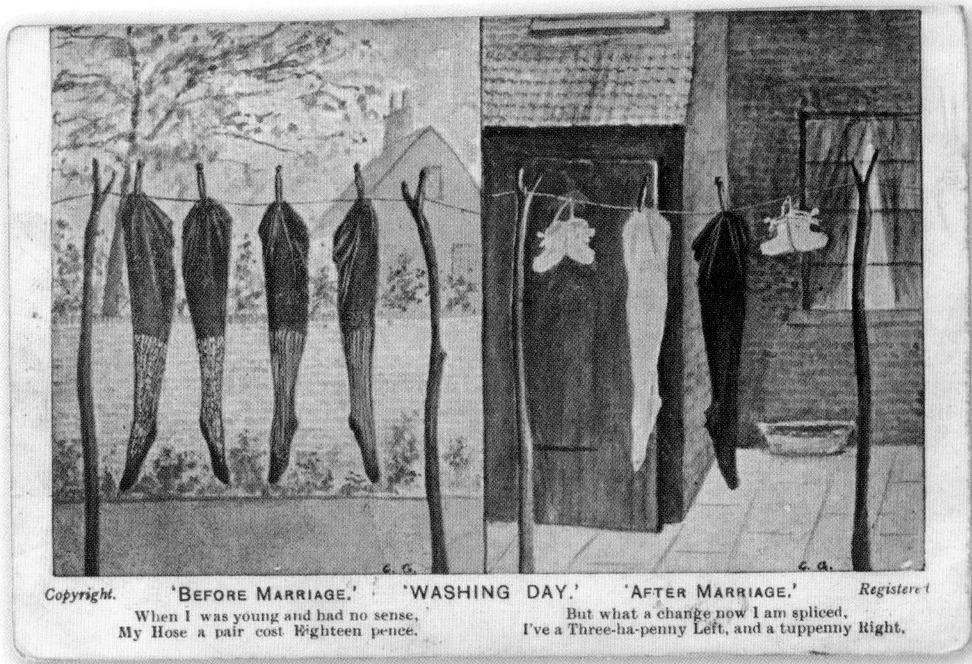
G. G.
G. G.
Copyright.
'BEFORE MARRIAGE.'
'WASHING DAY.'
'AFTER MARRIAGE.'
Registered
When I was young and had no sense,
My Hose a pair cost Eighteen pence.
But what a change now I am spliced,
I've a Three-ha-penny Left, and a tuppenny Right.

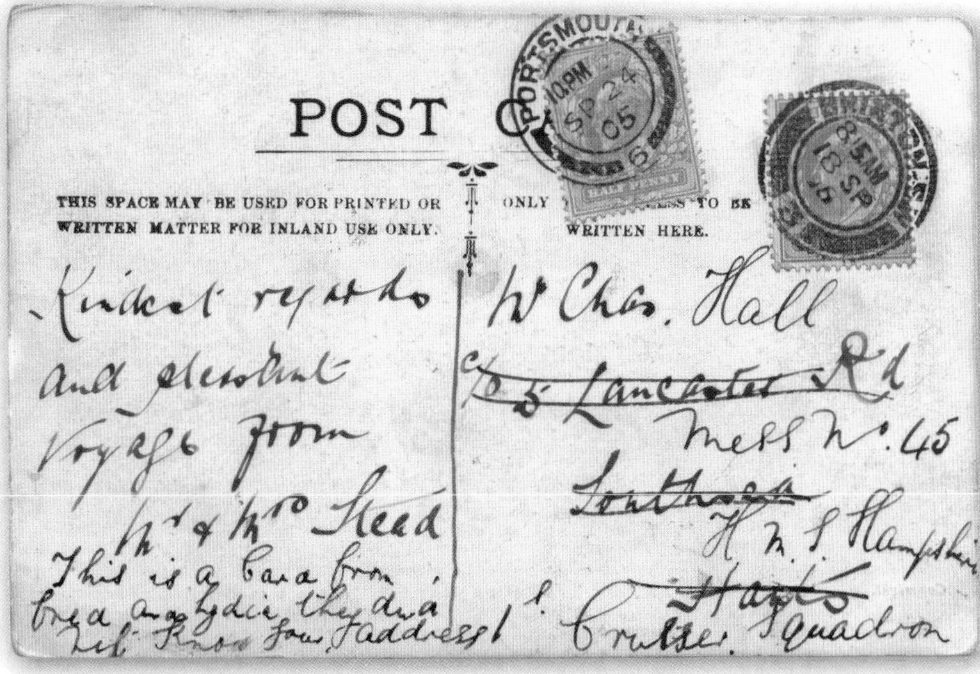
POST C
THIS SPACE MAY BE USED FOR PRINTED OR WRITTEN MATTER FOR INLAND USE ONLY.
ONLY
TO BE
WRITTEN HERE.
PORTSMOUTH
10 PM
SP 24
05
HALF PENNY
Kindest regards
and pleasant
voyage from
Mr & Mrs Steed
This is a card from
Mr Chas. Hall
5 Lancaster Rd
Mess No. 45
Southsea
H.M.S. Hampshire
Hants
1st Cruiser Squadron

Burns Monument, Ayr

RELIABLE SERIES.

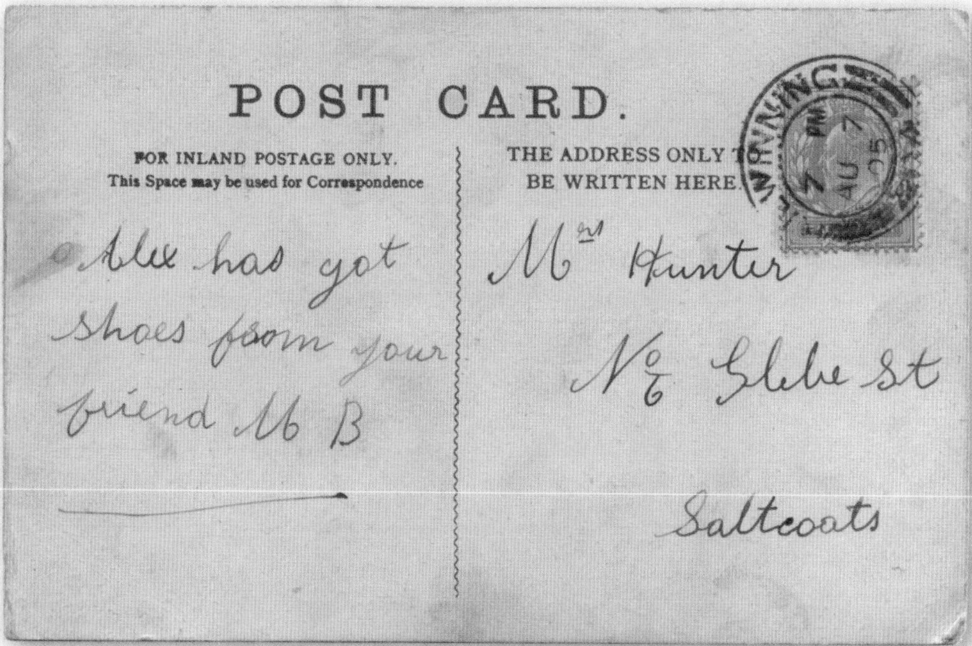

POST CARD.

FOR INLAND POSTAGE ONLY.
This Space may be used for Correspondence

Alex has got
shoes from your
friend M B

THE ADDRESS ONLY TO
BE WRITTEN HERE.

Mrs Hunter

No 6 Glebe St

Saltcoats

The Albert Memorial
F. G. O. Stuart. 868

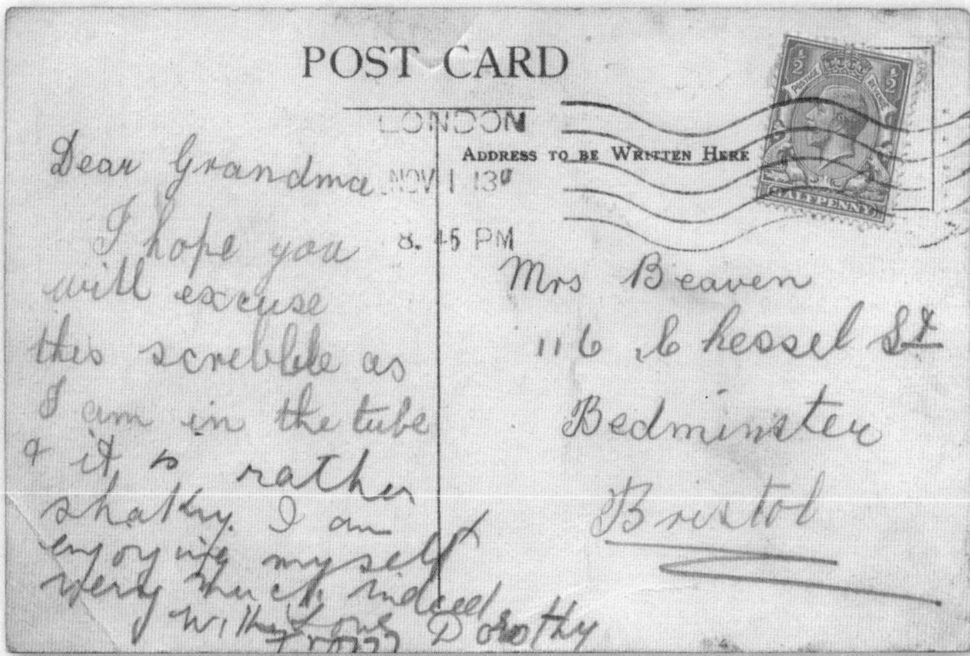

POST CARD

LONDON
NOV 1 13
8.45 PM

ADDRESS TO BE WRITTEN HERE

Dear Grandma
I hope you
will excuse
this scribble as
I am in the tube
& it is rather
shaky. I am
enjoying myself
very much indeed
with love from Dorothy

Mrs Beaven
116 Chessel St
Bedminster
Bristol

MISS PHYLLIS DARE. 761

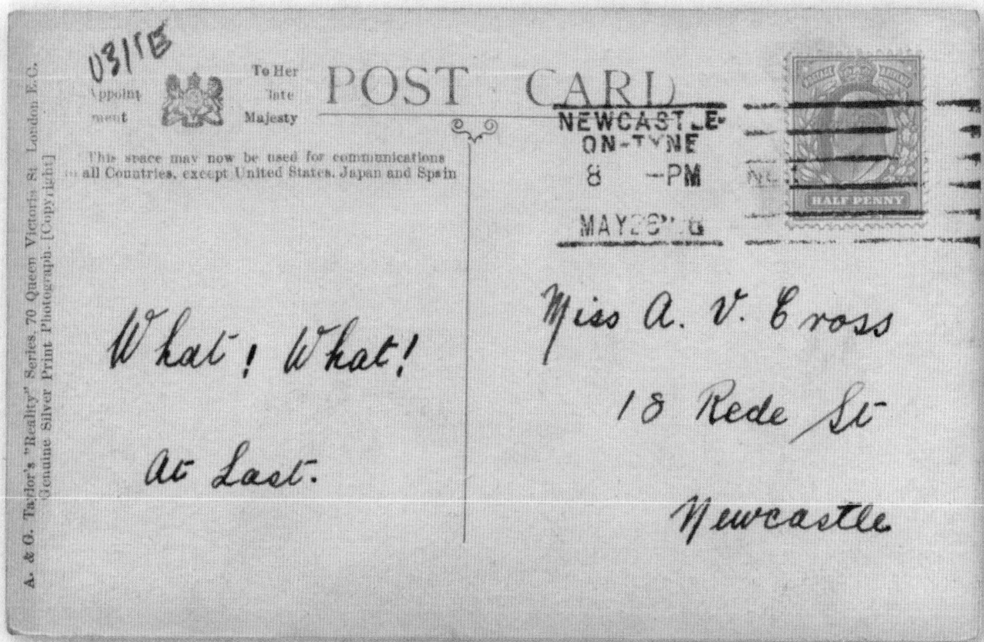
POST CARD
To Her Late Majesty
This space may now be used for communications to all Countries, except United States, Japan and Spain
A. & G. Taylor's "Reality" Series, 70 Queen Victoria St. London E.C.
Genuine Silver Print Photograph. [Copyright]
NEWCASTLE-ON-TYNE
8 -PM
HALF PENNY
What! What!
At Last.
Miss A. V. Cross
18 Rede St
Newcastle

Milton Lane, Portsmouth.
JWS 39

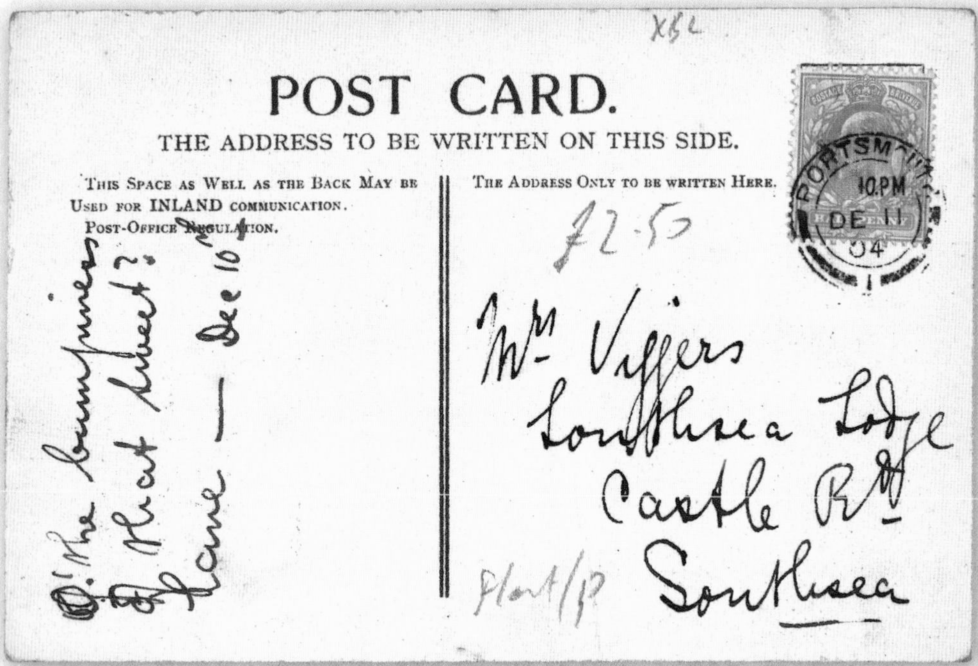
POST CARD.
THE ADDRESS TO BE WRITTEN ON THIS SIDE.
THIS SPACE AS WELL AS THE BACK MAY BE USED FOR INLAND COMMUNICATION. POST-OFFICE REGULATION.
THE ADDRESS ONLY TO BE WRITTEN HERE.
PORTSMOUTH 10.PM DE 11 04
Southsea Lodge
Castle Rd
Southsea

1457. 1.
Trinity College Bridge, Cambridge.

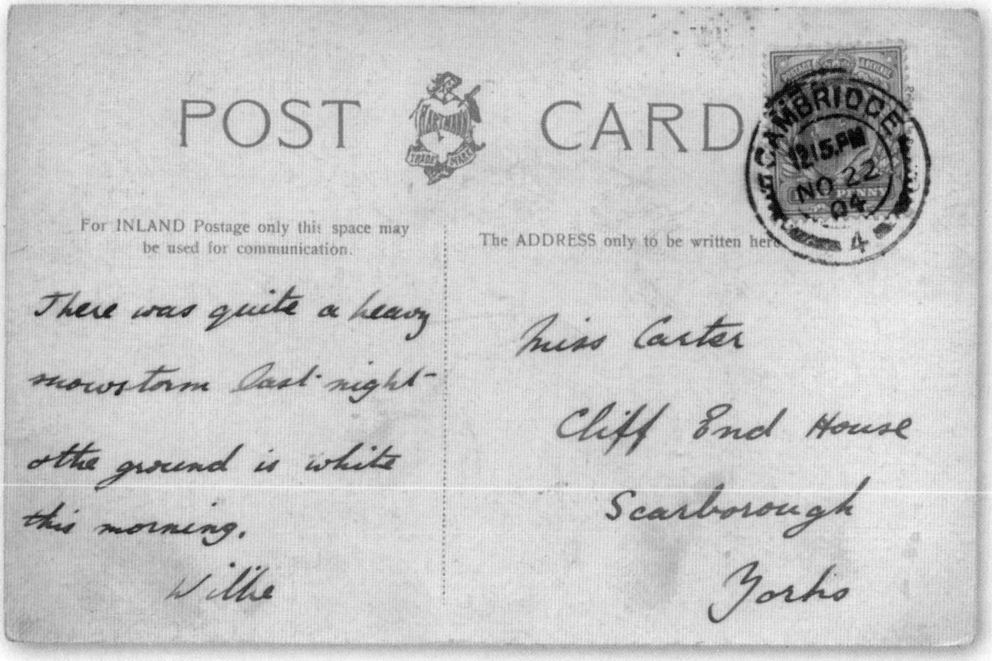
POST CARD
HARTMANN
TRADE MARK
CAMBRIDGE
12.15 PM
NO 22
04
4
For INLAND Postage only this space may be used for communication.
The ADDRESS only to be written here
There was quite a heavy snowstorm last night & the ground is white this morning.
Willie
Miss Carter
Cliff End House
Scarborough
Yorks

Yours truly
W. C. Hartley
May 1907.

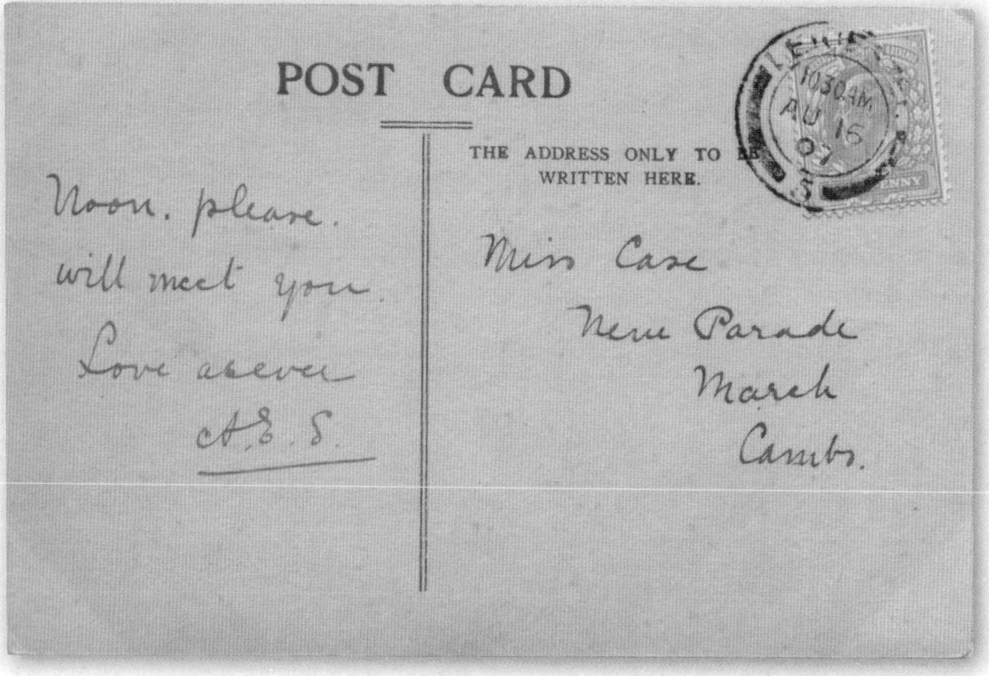
POST CARD

THE ADDRESS ONLY TO BE
WRITTEN HERE.

Noon. please.
will meet you.
Love as ever
A. E. S.

Miss Case
New Parade
March
Cambs.

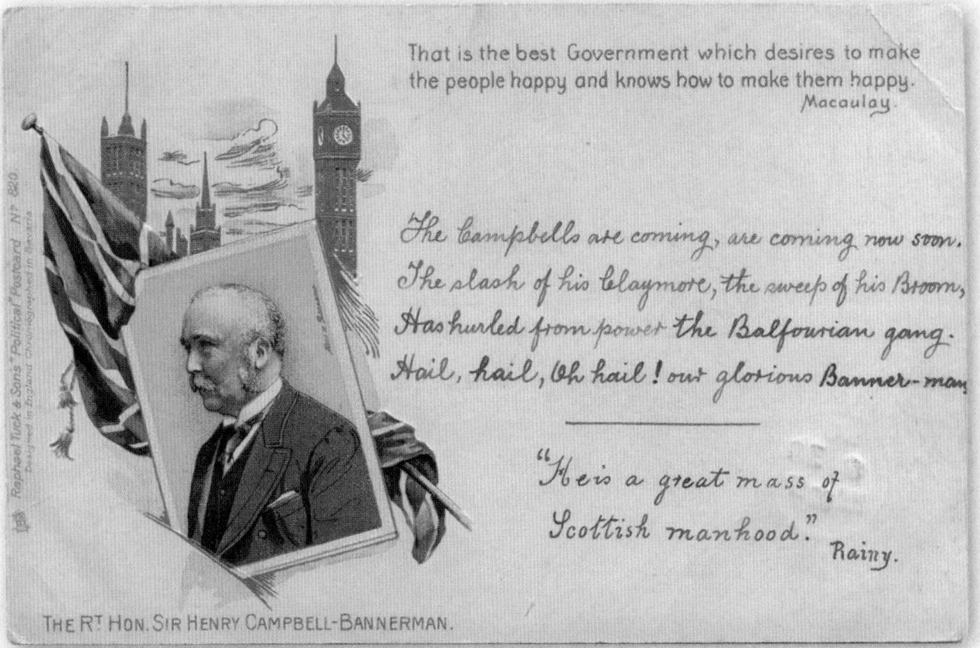
That is the best Government which desires to make the people happy and knows how to make them happy.
Macaulay.
The Campbells are coming, are coming now soon.
The slash of his Claymore, the sweep of his Broom,
Has hurled from power the Balfourian gang.
Hail, hail, Oh hail! our glorious Banner-man
"He is a great mass of Scottish manhood." Rainy.
Raphael Tuck & Sons' "Political" Postcard No 820.
Designed in England Chromographed in Bavaria
THE RT HON. SIR HENRY CAMPBELL-BANNERMAN.

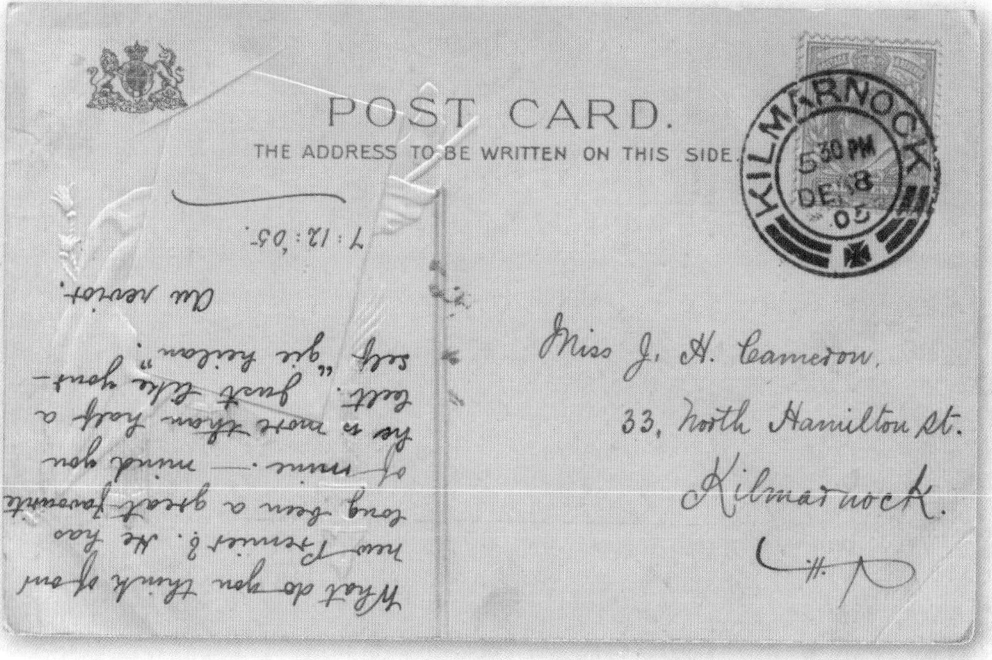
POST CARD.
THE ADDRESS TO BE WRITTEN ON THIS SIDE.
KILMARNOCK
5 30 PM
DE 8
05
Miss J. H. Cameron,
33, North Hamilton St.
Kilmarnock.
What do you think of our
new Premier?. He has
long been a great favourite
of mine. — mind you
he is more than half a
Celt. Just like your-
self "gie heilan".
Au revior.
7:12:'05.

WE WERE NOT A BIT DULL!

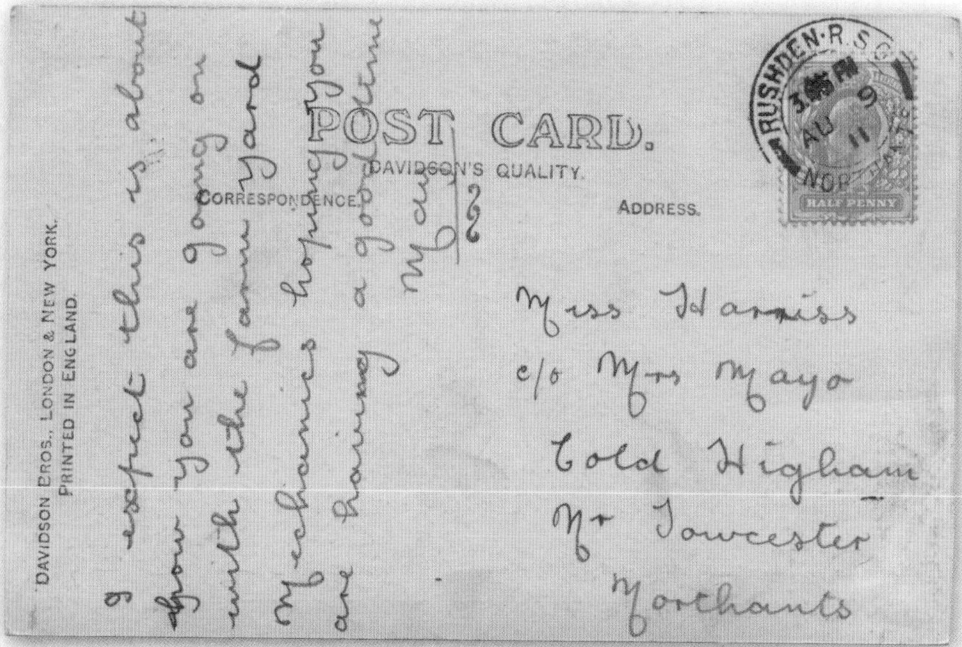
POST CARD.

DAVIDSON'S QUALITY.

CORRESPONDENCE. ADDRESS.

DAVIDSON BROS., LONDON & NEW YORK.
PRINTED IN ENGLAND.

I expect this is about
how you are going on
with the farm yard
Mechanics hoping you
are having a good time
May

Miss Harriss
c/o Mrs Mayo
Cold Higham
Nr Towcester
Northants

NOTTINGHAM GOOSE FAIR.
Copyright

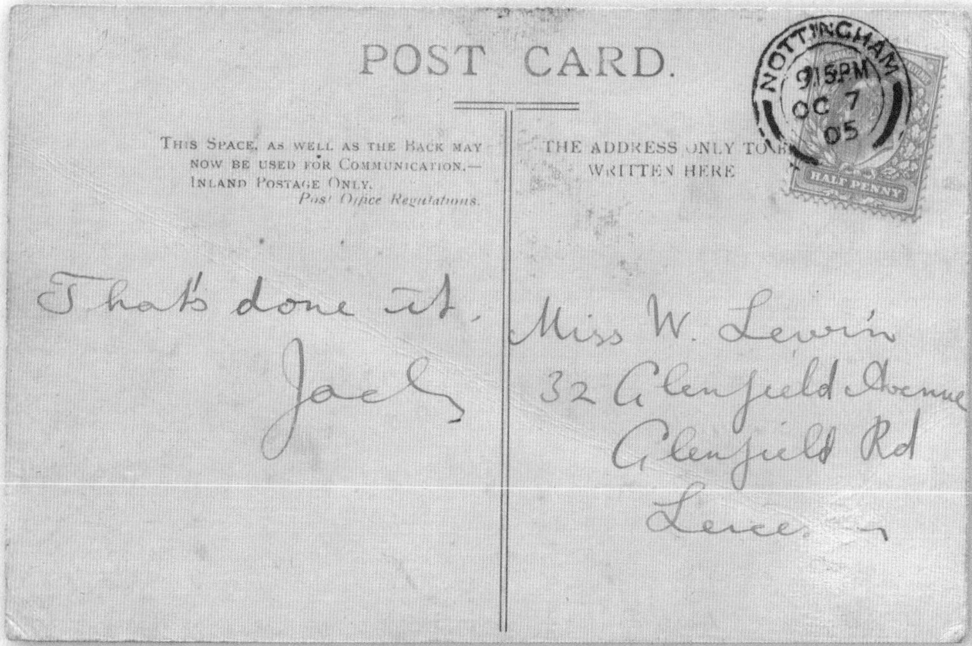

POST CARD.

THIS SPACE, AS WELL AS THE BACK MAY NOW BE USED FOR COMMUNICATION.— INLAND POSTAGE ONLY.
Post Office Regulations.

THE ADDRESS ONLY TO B
WRITTEN HERE

NOTTINGHAM
9.15 PM
OC 7
05

HALF PENNY

That's done it.
Jack

Miss W. Levin
32 Glenfield Avenue
Glenfield Rd
Leics.

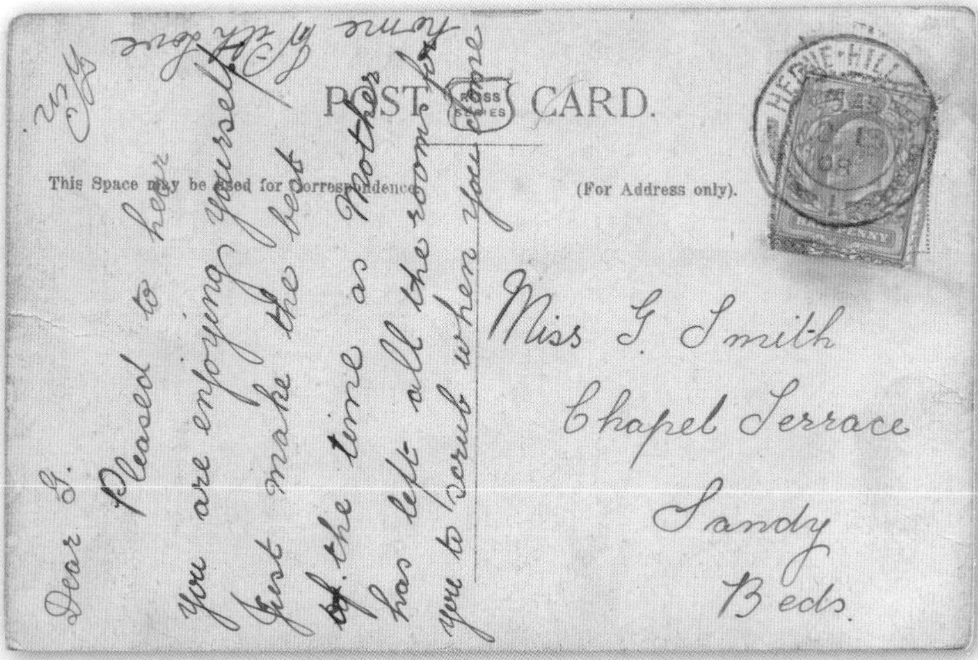
POST ROSS SERIES CARD.

This Space may be used for Correspondence

Dear G.
Pleased to hear
you are enjoying yourself
just make the best
of the time as Mother
has left all the rooms for
you to scrub when you come
home [illegible]

(For Address only).

Miss G. Smith
Chapel Terrace
Sandy
Beds.

THE HOSPITAL, BOSTON.

POST CARD.
This Space may be used for Correspondence.
The Address to be written here
E.T.W. Dennis & Sons Ltd. London & Scarborough
PRINTED IN ENGLAND
2677
£3.00
I'm very disappointed
no answer to my
letter - I must
know tomorrow
morn at the latest
what we are to
do so don't fail
to write today - Ev.
Miss M Barnes
Rushpool Hall
Saltburn by the
Sea

St. Mary's Abbey, York, from East.
RELIABLE SERIES

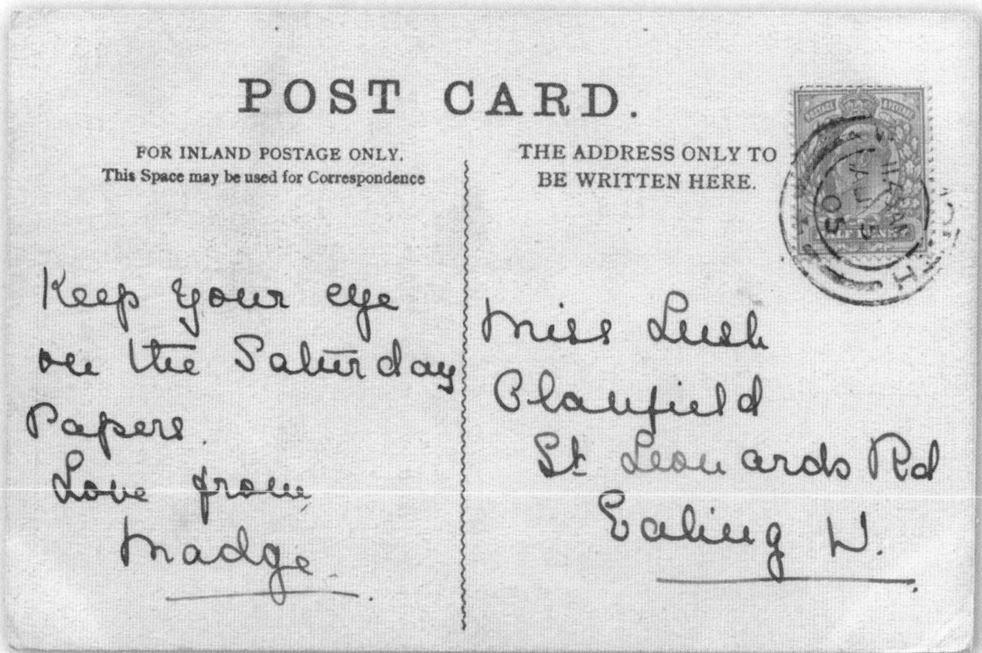

POST CARD.

FOR INLAND POSTAGE ONLY.
This Space may be used for Correspondence

THE ADDRESS ONLY TO
BE WRITTEN HERE.

Keep your eye
on the Saturday
papers.
Love from
Madge

Miss Lush
Clanfield
St Leonards Rd
Ealing W.

HARZ
RIEFENBACHTHAL.

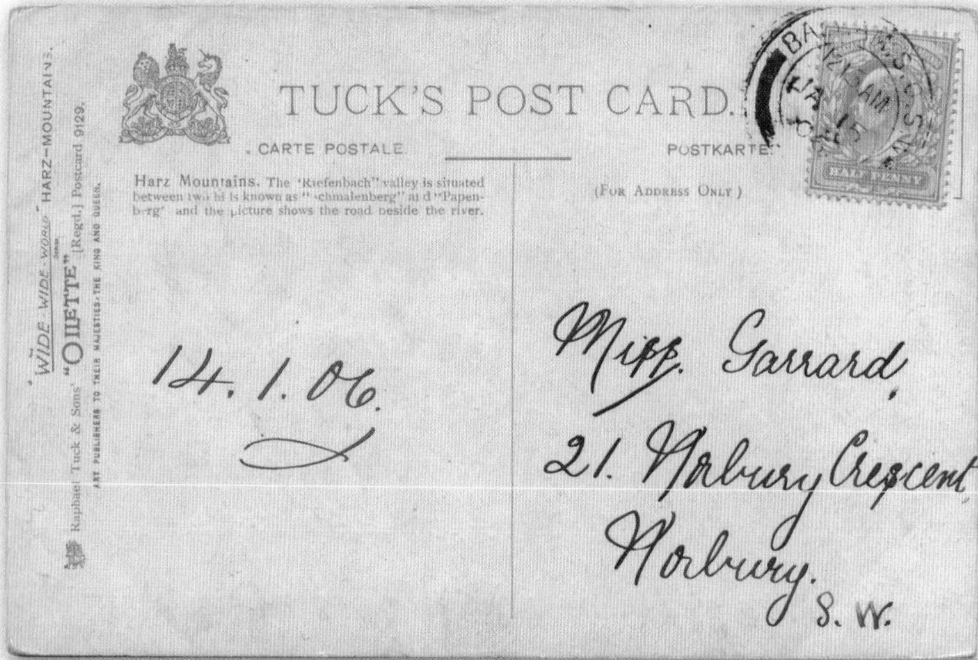
"WIDE-WIDE-WORLD" Series HARZ-MOUNTAINS.

Raphael Tuck & Sons' "OILETTE" [Regd.] Postcard 9129.

ART PUBLISHERS TO THEIR MAJESTIES THE KING AND QUEEN.

TUCK'S POST CARD.

CARTE POSTALE POSTKARTE

Harz Mountains. The 'Riefenbach" valley is situated between two hi ls known as "ʻchmalenberg" and "Papenberg" and the picture shows the road beside the river.

(FOR ADDRESS ONLY.)

HALF PENNY

14. 1. 06.

Miss. Garrard,

21. Norbury Crescent

Norbury.

S. W.

George Street, Edinburgh.
1050. 35.

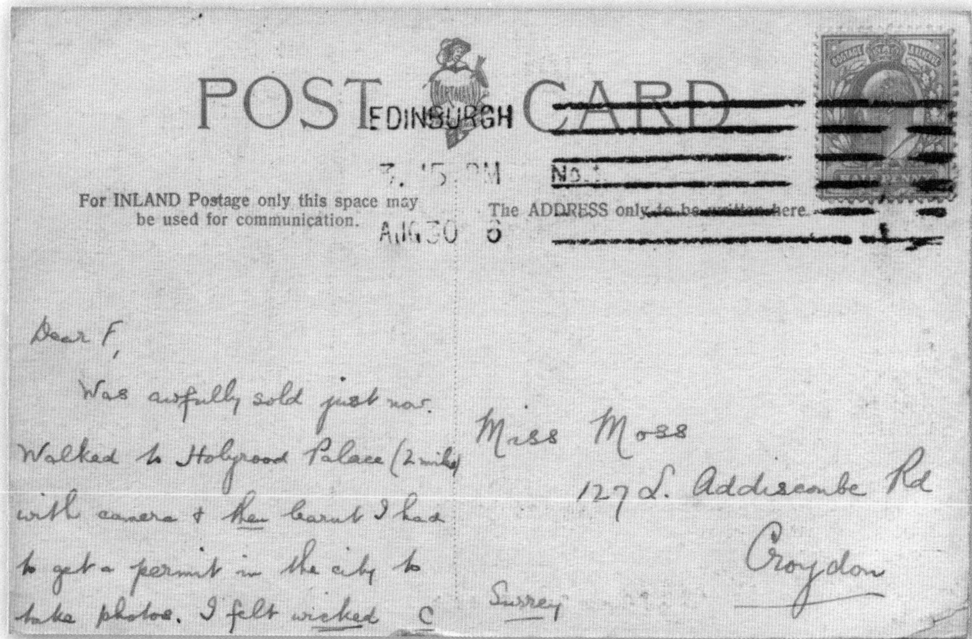
POST CARD

EDINBURGH 7.15 PM AUG 30 6

For INLAND Postage only this space may be used for communication.

The ADDRESS only to be written here.

Dear F,

Was awfully sold just now. Walked to Holyrood Palace (2 miles) with camera & then learnt I had to get a permit in the city to take photos. I felt wicked C

Miss Moss

127 L. Addiscombe Rd

Croydon

Surrey

CRAGSIDE NEAR ROTHBURY.
Copyright.

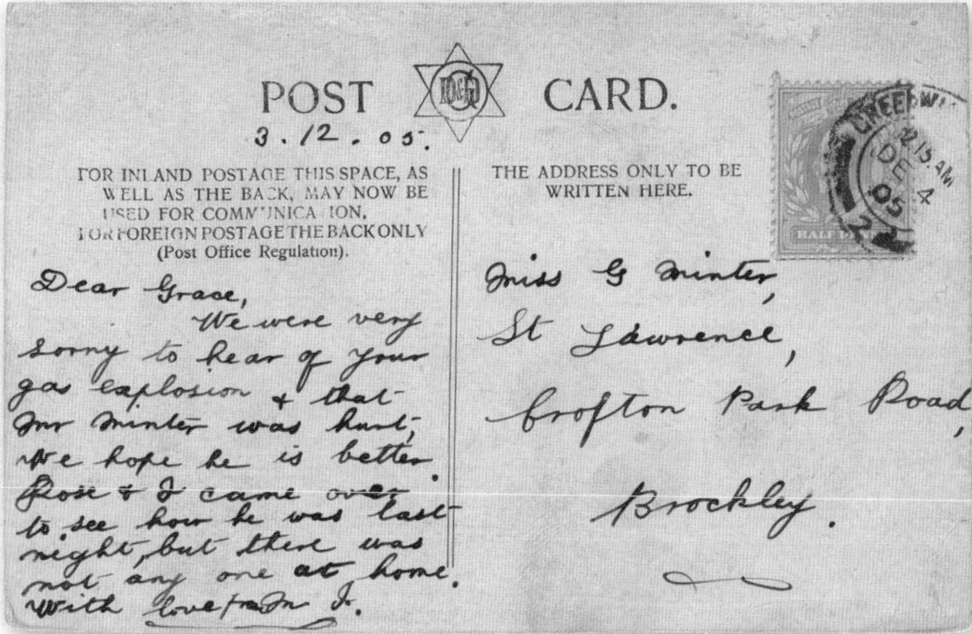

POST CARD.

3.12.05.

FOR INLAND POSTAGE THIS SPACE, AS WELL AS THE BACK, MAY NOW BE USED FOR COMMUNICATION.
FOR FOREIGN POSTAGE THE BACK ONLY
(Post Office Regulation).

Dear Grace,
We were very sorry to hear of your gas explosion & that Mr Minter was hurt; we hope he is better. Rose & I came over to see how he was last night, but there was not any one at home.
With love from J.

THE ADDRESS ONLY TO BE WRITTEN HERE.

Miss G Minter,
St Lawrence,
Crofton Park Road,
Brockley.

ST MARK'S CHURCH, REGENT'S PARK

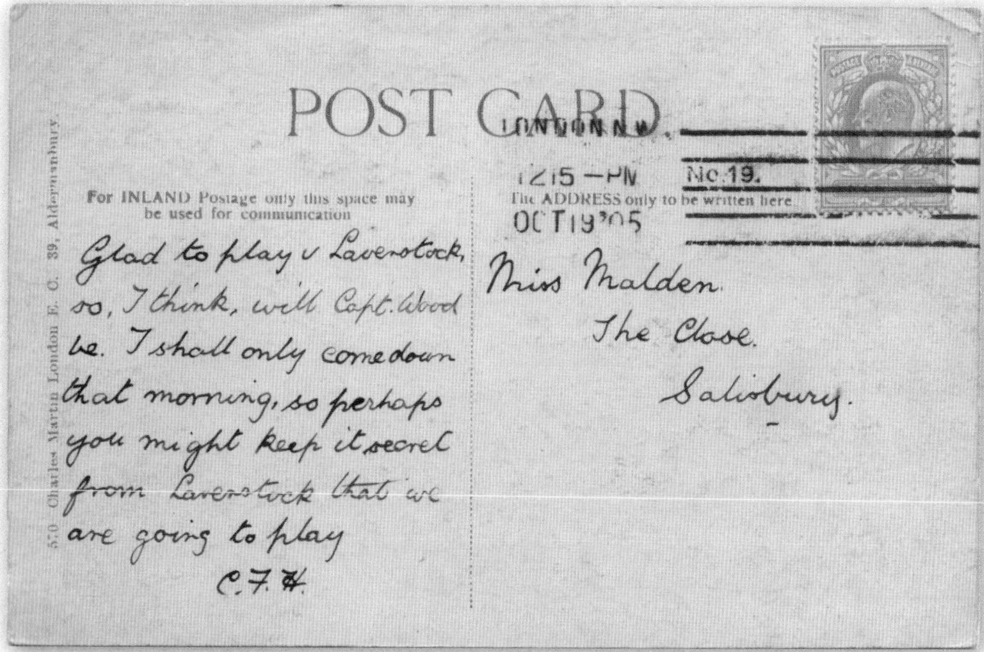

570 Charles Martin London E.C. 39, Aldermanbury.

POST CARD.

For INLAND Postage only this space may be used for communication

The ADDRESS only to be written here.

LONDON N.W. 12.15 – PM OCT 19 '05 No 19.

Glad to play v Laverstock, so, I think, will Capt. Wood be. I shall only come down that morning, so perhaps you might keep it secret from Laverstock that we are going to play

C.F.H.

Miss Malden.
The Close.
Salisbury.

SAND ARTISTS.
Z 1507

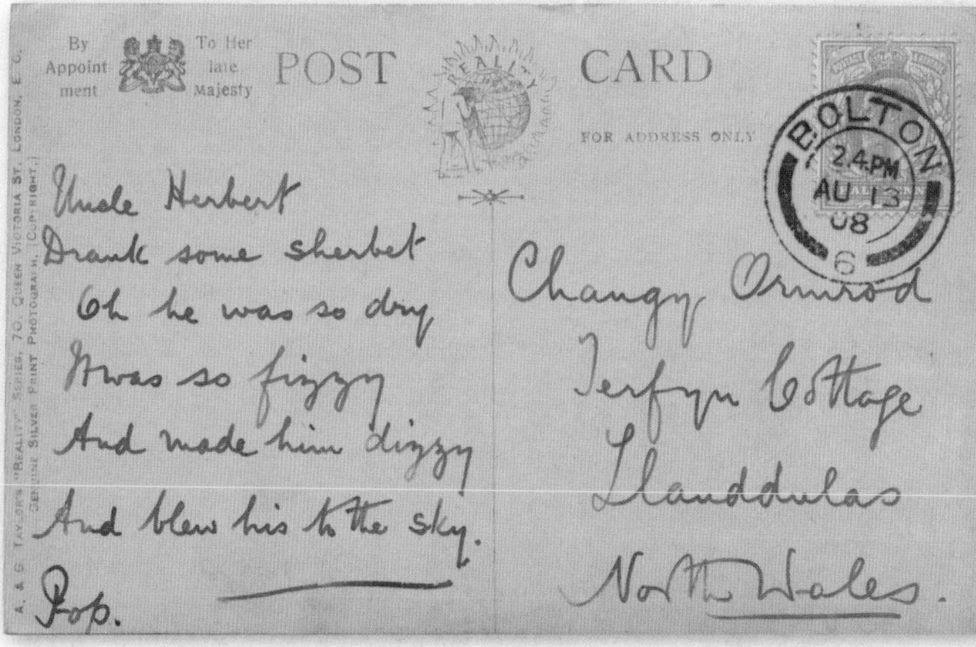

A. & G. TAYLOR'S "REALITY" SERIES, 70, QUEEN VICTORIA ST, LONDON, E.C.
GENUINE SILVER PRINT PHOTOGRAPH. (COPYRIGHT.)

By Appointment To Her late Majesty

POST CARD

FOR ADDRESS ONLY

BOLTON
2.4 PM
AU 13
08
6

Uncle Herbert
Drank some sherbet
Oh he was so dry
It was so fizzy
And made him dizzy
And blew his to the sky.
Pop.

Changy Ormrod
Tenfryn Cottage
Llanddulas
North Wales.

THE SCOTTISH WIDOWS' FUND
BLACK AND WHITE
BEECHAMS PILLS
For Bilious Attac
HAVE YOU A RED NOSE
MOTHER SEIGEL'S SYRUP
NICELY PROPORTIONED WOMEN.
ANTIPON
Full Up
Homward Bound.
F. Wright
1910
New Years Day

Pre 1910

POST CARD. £5

For the British Isles only, THIS SPACE AS WELL AS THE BACK MAY BE USED FOR CORRESPONDENCE.

THE ADDRESS ONLY TO BE WRITTEN HERE.

GRAVESEND
12 PM
25
10

Mrs Wright
13 Milton Road
Waterloo
Liverpool
England

Highlow Hall, Hathersage

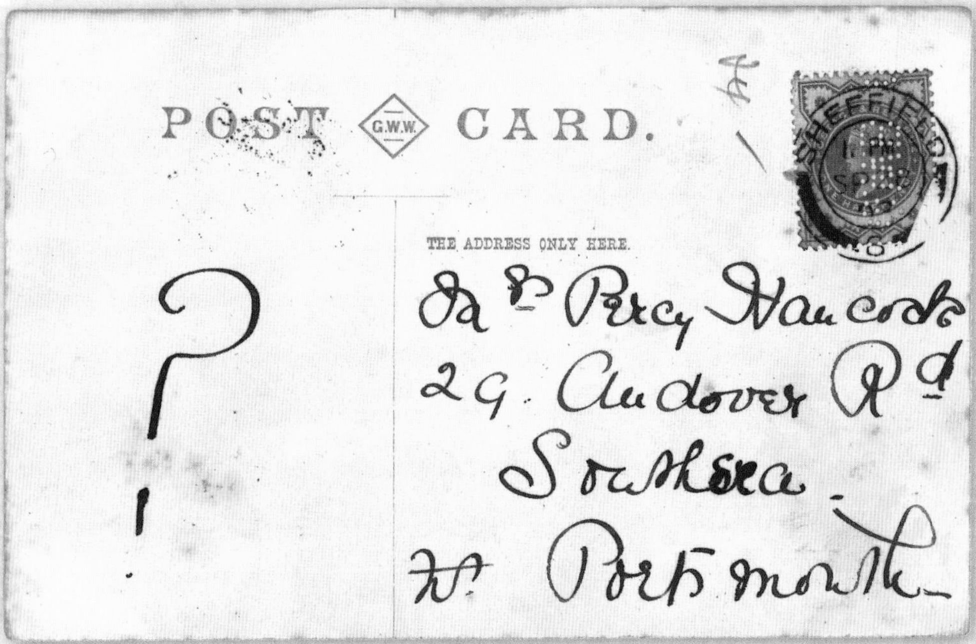
POST G.W.W. CARD.
THE ADDRESS ONLY HERE.
SHEFFIELD
Percy Hancock
29 Andover Rd
Southsea
Portsmouth
?

SANDLING JUNCTION STATION,
SOUTH EASTERN & CHATHAM RAILWAY.

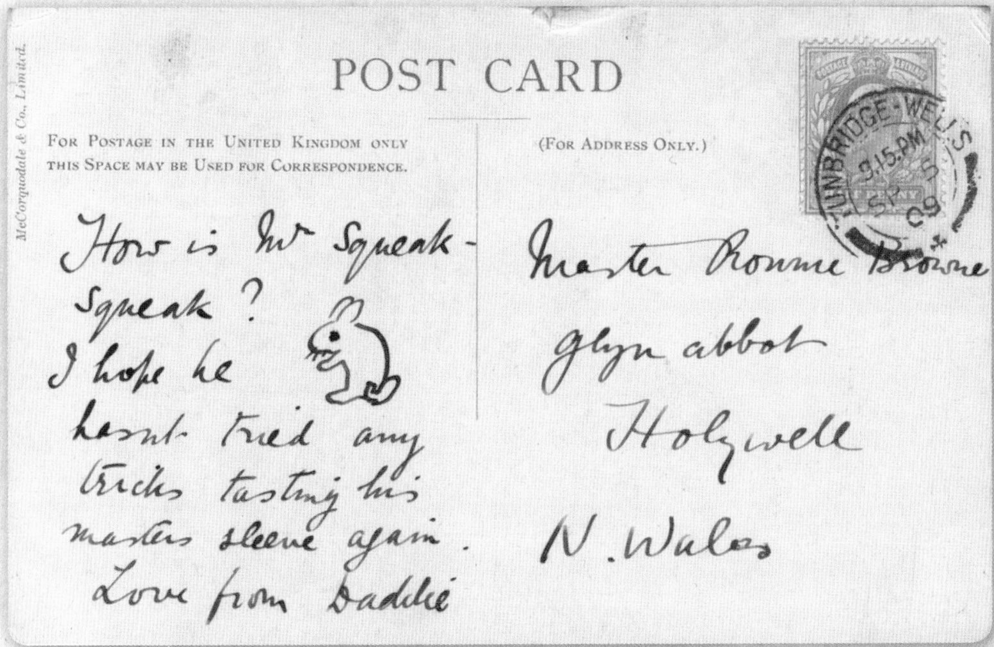
McCorquodale & Co., Limited.

POST CARD

FOR POSTAGE IN THE UNITED KINGDOM ONLY
THIS SPACE MAY BE USED FOR CORRESPONDENCE.

(FOR ADDRESS ONLY.)

TUNBRIDGE-WELLS
9.15 PM
SP 5
09

How is Mr Squeak-
Squeak?
I hope he
hasn't tried any
tricks tasting his
masters sleeve again.
Love from Daddie

Master Ronnie Browne
Glyn abbot
Holywell
N. Wales

Series 5036 - 4
THE EMBANKMENT, LONDON.
Davidson Brothers
LONDON.

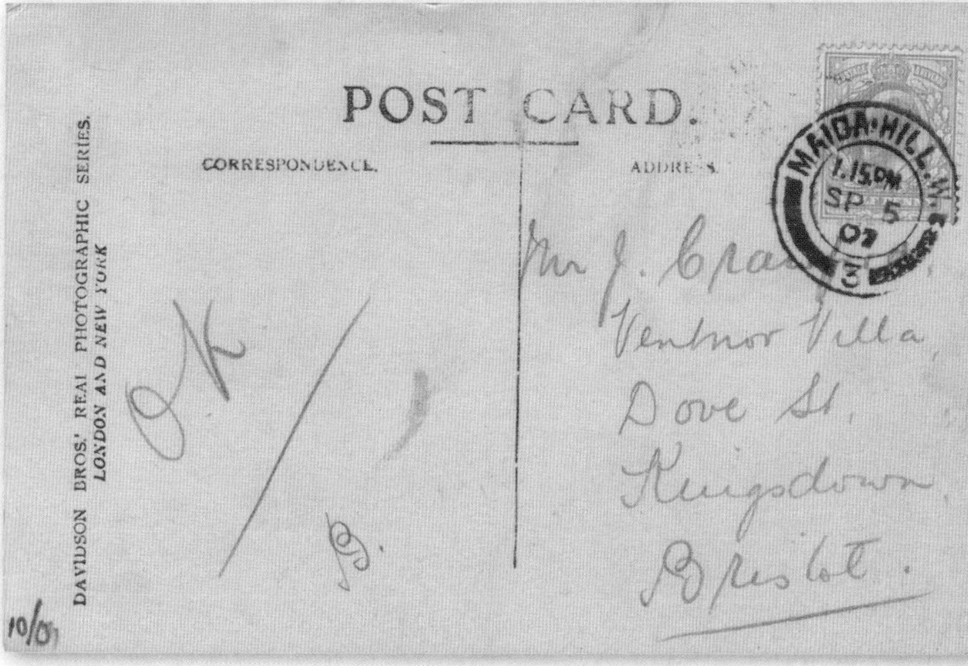
POST CARD.
CORRESPONDENCE.
ADDRESS.
DAVIDSON BROS.' REAL PHOTOGRAPHIC SERIES.
LONDON AND NEW YORK
MAIDA·HILL.W.
1.15 PM
SP 5
07
3
Ventnor Villa,
Dove St,
Kingsdown,
Bristol.

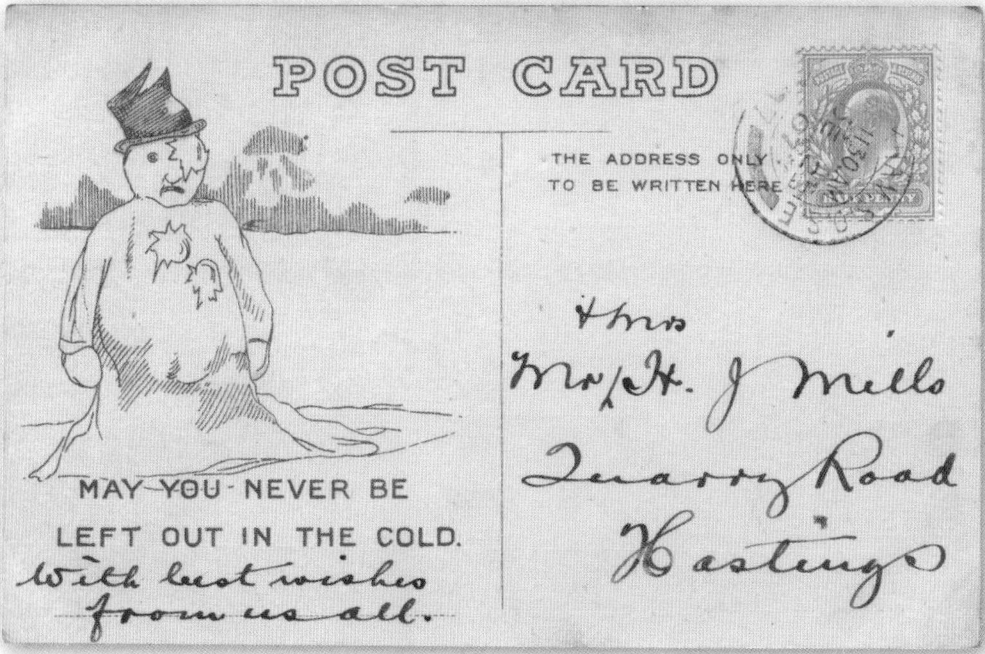
POST CARD
THE ADDRESS ONLY
TO BE WRITTEN HERE
MAY YOU NEVER BE
LEFT OUT IN THE COLD.
With best wishes
from us all.
& Mrs
Mr H. J Mills
Quarry Road
Hastings

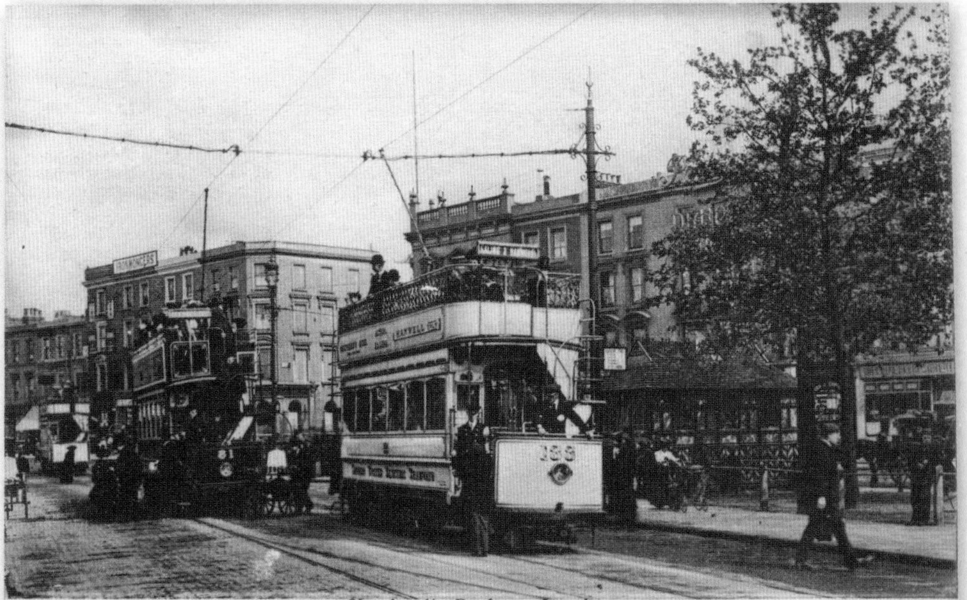

Shepherd's Bush – London

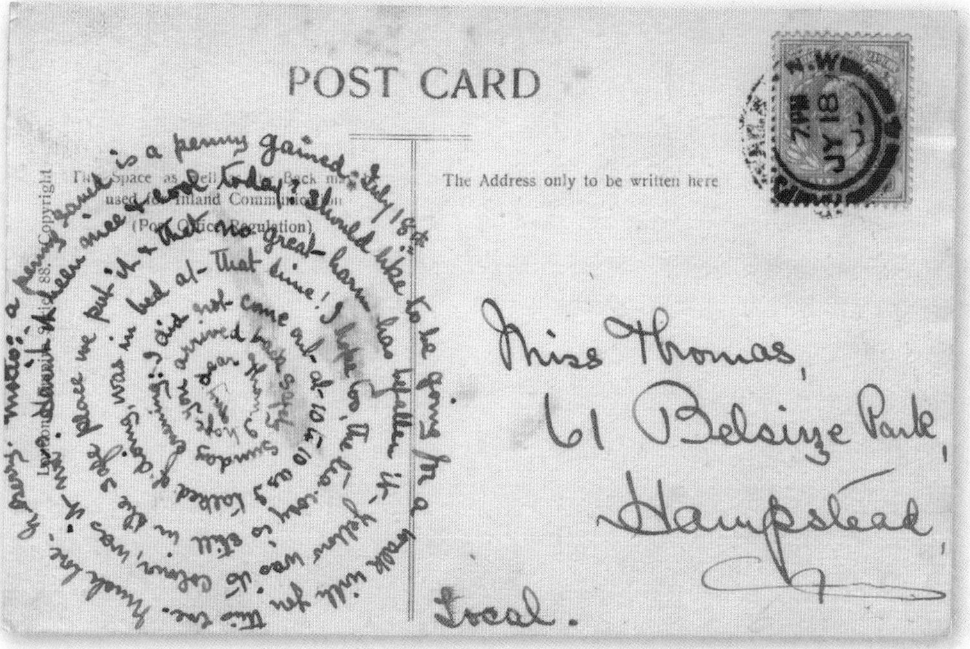
POST CARD
The Address only to be written here
used for Inland Communication
(Post Office Regulation)
Miss Thomas,
61 Belsize Park,
Hampstead
Local.

Bizet

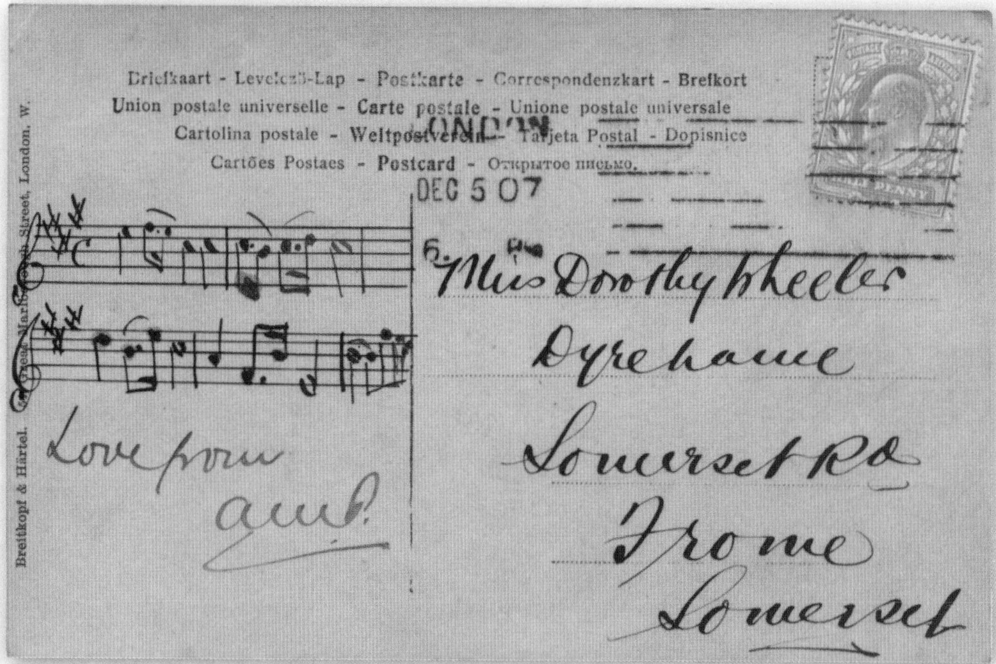
Briefkaart - Levelező-Lap - Postkarte - Correspondenzkart - Brefkort
Union postale universelle - Carte postale - Unione postale universale
Cartolina postale - Weltpostverein - Tarjeta Postal - Dopisnice
Cartões Postaes - Postcard - Открытое письмо.
DEC 5 07
Breitkopf & Härtel.
London. W.
Miss Dorothy Wheeler
Somerset Rd
Frome
Somerset
Love from
aunt

BROAD STREET, READING.
READING

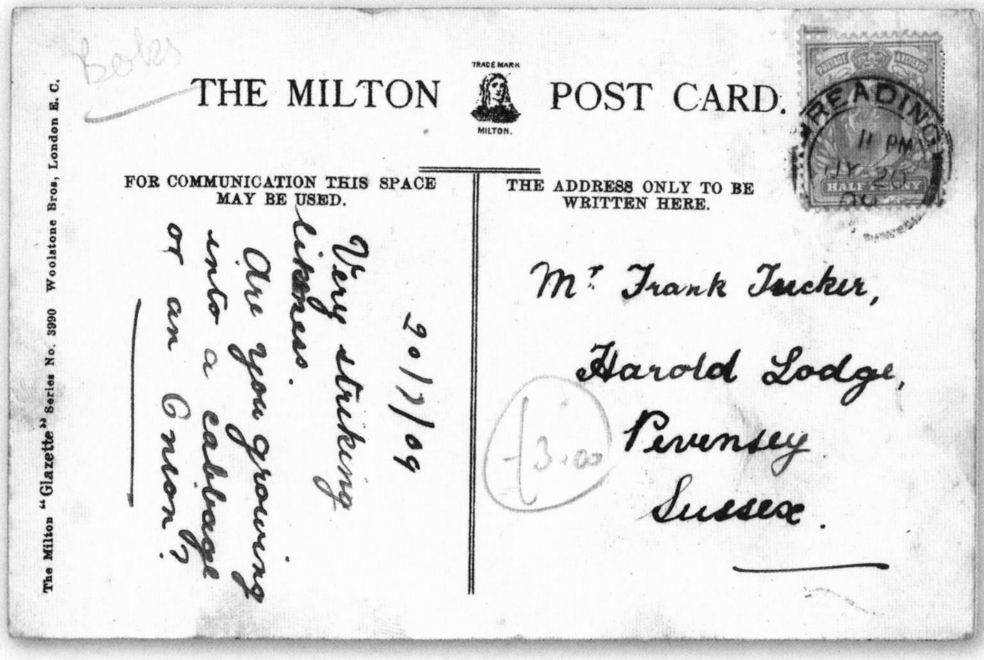
THE MILTON POST CARD.

TRADE MARK MILTON.

FOR COMMUNICATION THIS SPACE MAY BE USED.

20/7/09

Very striking likeness.

Are you growing into a cabbage or an Onion?

THE ADDRESS ONLY TO BE WRITTEN HERE.

Mr. Frank Tucker,

Harold Lodge,

Pevensey,

Sussex.

READING 11 PM JY 20 09

HALF PENNY

The Milton "Glazette" Series No. 3990 Woolstone Bros, London E. C.

PALLING BEACH.
AUG 20 '04
We have been having dinner along here, & are now going to walk on.
Arthur V. Prior
Mary
Lucy.

GERMANY
Postkarte
An Mrs Prior
The Red House
in Harrow.
Wohnung
(Strasse und Hausnummer.)

"ALL FOR YOU."

B. & D. LONDON E.C.

"KROMO" SERIES No 21587

POST CARD

WRITING SPACE.

TRADE MARK.

NAME AND ADDRESS.

NEWQUAY
A
JA 20
07

Dear Martin
thanks for the
post card, I started
school on Thursday
with best love from
Ethel xxxxxxxxxxxxxxx

Mr M Sandberg
Schr Katie
Runcorn
Cheshire

4122 F ROTARY PHOTO, E.C.
MISS PHYLLIS DARE.
FOULSHAM & BANFIELD

POST CARD.
THE ADDRESS ONLY TO BE WRITTEN HERE.
LONDON E.C. 3 OCT PM 1907
ROTARY PHOTOGRAPHIC SERIES.
Miss L. Simmonds
694 Wandsworth Rd.
S.W.

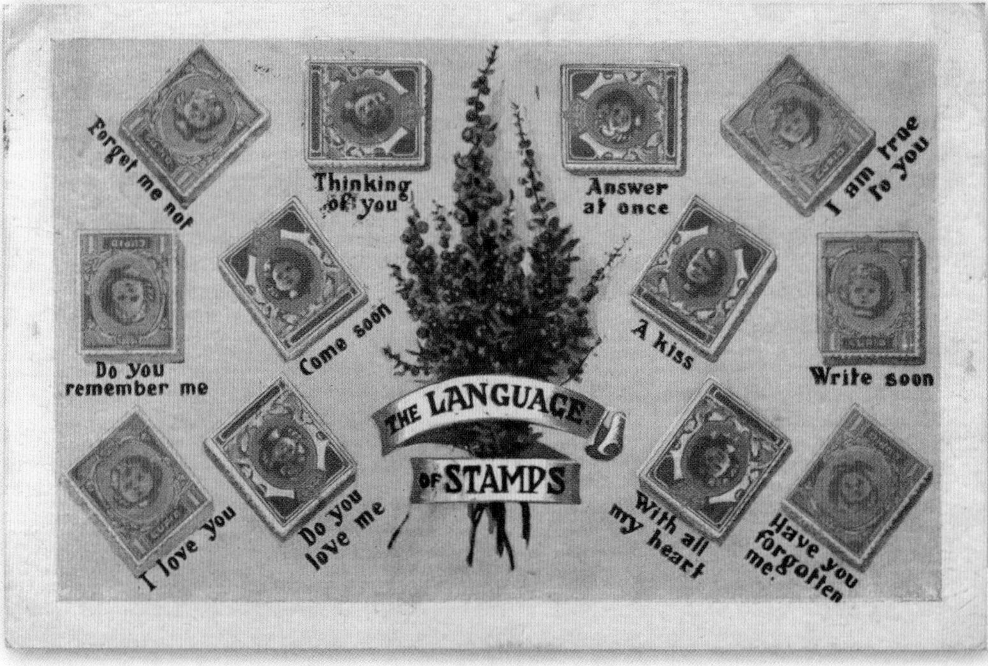
THE LANGUAGE OF STAMPS
Forget me not
Thinking of you
Answer at once
I am true to you
Do you remember me
Come soon
A kiss
Write soon
I love you
Do you love me
With all my heart
Have you forgotten me

P.S.

Take care affixing your stamps…

Just as the cards in this book suggest, many Edwardians felt comfortable using postcards for sending the most intimate of messages. And it wasn't just the sender's words or the postcard's picture that were deployed to signal affection. An angled stamp was widely known to demonstrate love towards the recipient, or at least to lighten the tone of a message: it was, you could say, the Edwardian emoticon or smiley face. Guides to 'The Language of Stamps' were published on cards like the one on the opposite page – although such cards were not definitive. After all, the best codes are understood by only the sender and the recipient.

P.P.S.

Did you spot the hidden question on the front of the card on p.54? To 'read it', shut one of your eyes, lift up the page slightly, and look down the card from its shorter side, towards the centre of the book.

Acknowledgements

I would like to thank lots of people for encouraging and helping me to put this book together, especially Helen, my parents, Ben, Andrea, Alvin, David, John, Michael, Mark, Fiona, Hafiz, Jo, Isabella, Suzanne, Hedley, Julia, Brian, Matt, Annebella, Dave, Tim, Paul, Emma, Laura, Alison, Sally, Jake, Nigel, Susan, and Michelle.

I am also grateful for the assistance of WH Smith plc, the Francis Frith Collection, the archive of James Valentine & Sons held by the University of St Andrews, and the British Postal Museum & Archive.

Most importantly, I am indebted to all the senders, recipients, collectors and dealers whose hands the postcards have passed through over the years. It would, of course, be wonderful if people with stories about the cards were to get in touch. It is easiest to contact me through my blog **www.postcardese.blogspot.com**.

If you would like to begin collecting, details of clubs and fairs in the UK can be found on the Postcard Traders Association website **www.postcard.co.uk**, or in *Picture Postcard Monthly*. But be careful, once you start…

About the Author

Guy Atkins is a writer and researcher based in London. He read Philosophy, Politics and Economics at Oriel College, Oxford and holds an MA in Art and Politics from Goldsmiths, University of London. After ten years working in and around the civil service, Guy has returned to academia. He is currently undertaking a PhD at Goldsmiths and the Museum of London. He writes a monthly column on collecting postcards in *Stamp & Coin Mart* magazine, and regularly speaks about the history of postcards at clubs and societies across the UK.